Cyanide & Happiness™
STAB FACTORY

Kris, Rob & Dave

BOOM! BOX™

Designers Kara Leopard & Michelle Ankley
Associate Editor Jasmine Amiri
Editors Shannon Watters & Bryce Carlson

BOOM! BOX™

ROSS RICHIE CEO & Founder • MATT GAGNON Editor-in-Chief • FILIP SABLIK President of Publishing & Marketing • STEPHEN CHRISTY President of Development • LANCE KREITER VP of Licensing & Merchandising
PHIL BARBARO VP of Finance • BRYCE CARLSON Managing Editor • MEL CAYLO Marketing Manager • SCOTT NEWMAN Production Design Manager • IRENE BRADISH Operations Manager • CHRISTINE DINH Brand Communications Manager
SIERRA HAHN Senior Editor • DAFNA PLEBAN Editor • SHANNON WATTERS Editor • ERIC HARBURN Editor • IAN BRILL Editor • WHITNEY LEOPARD Associate Editor • JASMINE AMIRI Associate Editor • CHRIS ROSA Associate Editor
ALEX GALER Assistant Editor • CAMERON CHITTOCK Assistant Editor • MARY GUMPORT Assistant Editor • KELSEY DIETERICH Production Designer • JILLIAN CRAB Production Designer • KARA LEOPARD Production Designer
MICHELLE ANKLEY Production Design Assistant • DEVIN FUNCHES E-Commerce & Inventory Coordinator • AARON FERRARA Operations Coordinator • JOSÉ MEZA Sales Assistant • JAMES ARRIOLA Mailroom Assistant
ELIZABETH LOUGHRIDGE Accounting Assistant • STEPHANIE HOCUTT Marketing Assistant • SAM KUSEK Direct Market Representative • HILLARY LEVI Executive Assistant • KATE ALBIN Administrative Assistant

A catalog record of this book is available from OCLC and from the BOOM! Studios website, www.boom-studios.com, on the Librarians Page.

For other Cyanide & Happiness comics, animated shorts, books, and merchandise, visit www.explosm.net

BOOM! Studios, 5670 Wilshire Boulevard, Suite 450, Los Angeles, CA 90036-5679. Printed in China. First Printing. ISBN: 978-1-60886-769-1, eISBN: 978-1-61398-440-6

Dedicated to God.

FOREWORD

I can remember it like it was yesterday. Pop was out gathering firewood for the winter while Mother stayed inside, tending as best she could to the lilacs wilting in the kitchen window. I was sitting on the cold tile playing with a wooden hoop by Mother's feet. It was then, with Mother by the lilacs and I by her feet, that my dear sister Bedelia burst in to the kitchen:

"Mother! Brother! I've just found the most wonderful thing!"

"What is it, Bedelia?" Mother moaned.

"Well," Bedelia answered, "you know how the internet has become neutered and corporatized? And that the only people fighting that corporatization are anarchic sociopaths? So, the internet has been reduced to a fight between soulless media conglomerates and entitled misanthropes?"

"Sure, I do!" Mother moaned louder.

"Well, I found this comic! It's called Cyanide & Happiness. It's smart and funny and sad and touching and horrifying and lovely and depressing—sometimes all at the same time!"

"Like life!" I said, saying my first words ever.

"Exactly!" Bedelia exclaimed, "C&H is a beacon of hope. A symbol of what the internet could have been—and still could be! A comic done by people, for the people, to the people, through the people. Hilarious, subversive, clever, unapologetic art. Art that could have only been made now. Because it is now. Do you understand Mother? Brother? The internet can be a wonderful place. Just as long as Cyanide & Happiness keep doing good work."

"And as long as they stay on the internet." I replied. "And don't do something stupid like, you know, print out their comics and put them in a dying medium."

"They wouldn't do that," Bedelia asserted.

But she was wrong. And Pop came inside shortly after. The firewood was rotten and unusable. It was going to be a long winter.

BO BURNHAM

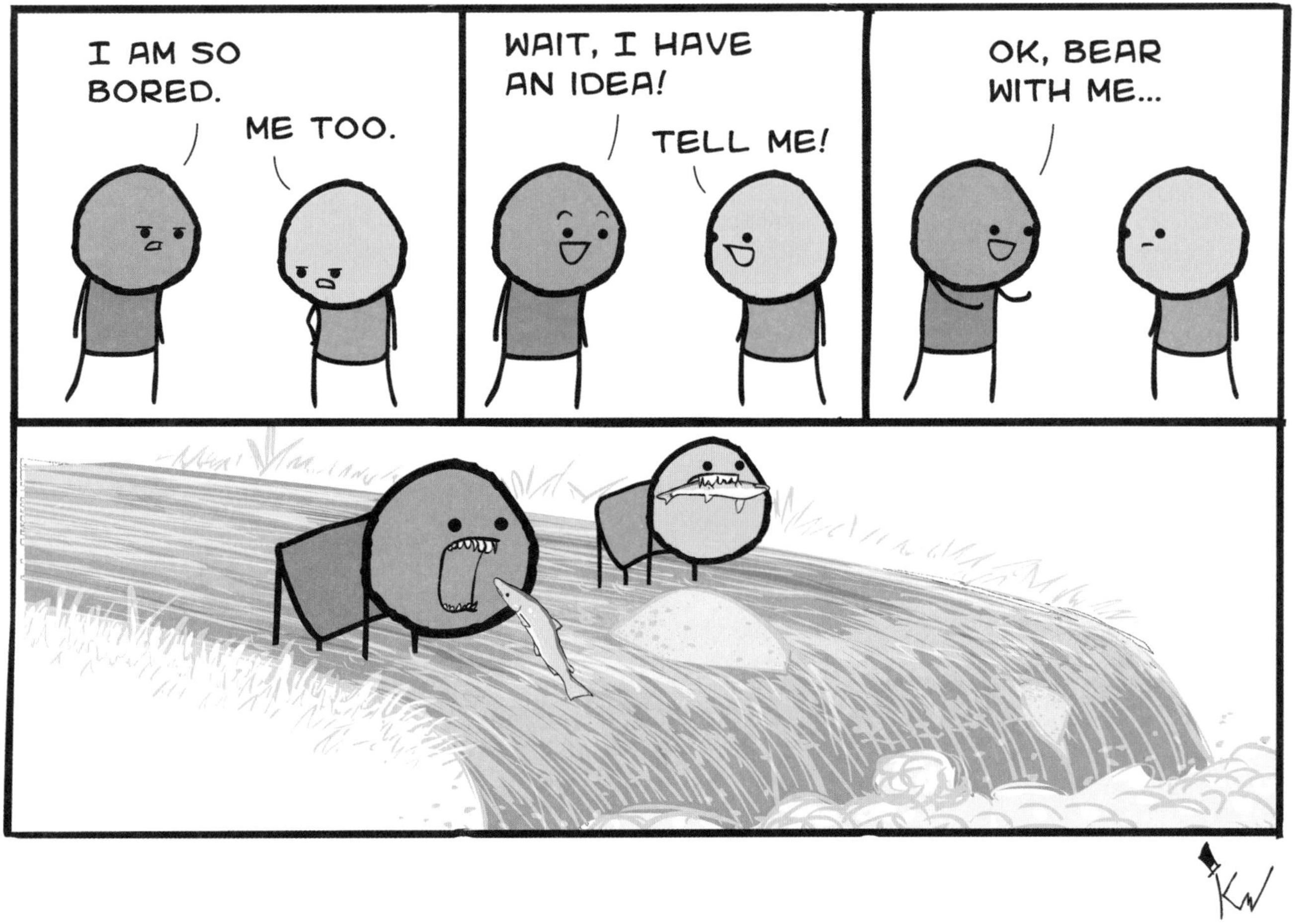
I AM SO BORED.
ME TOO.
WAIT, I HAVE AN IDEA!
TELL ME!
OK, BEAR WITH ME...

READY FOR THE **KNIFE FIGHT?!**

YEAH... I BROUGHT A **GUN** TO YOUR KNIFE FIGHT!

WELL I BROUGHT A **GRENADE** TO YOUR **GUN FIGHT!**

YEAH? I BROUGHT A **FLAMETHROWER** TO YOUR GRENADE FIGHT!

WHOA, WHOA. I FEEL LIKE THIS IS JUST BECOMING AN ARMS RACE.

I BROUGHT A **LEG** TO YOUR ARMS RACE!

WHAT'S WRONG WITH ME, GOOGLE DOC?
WELL, WE GOT YOUR RESULTS BACK..
THERE'S 18,300,000 OF THEM.
Dave

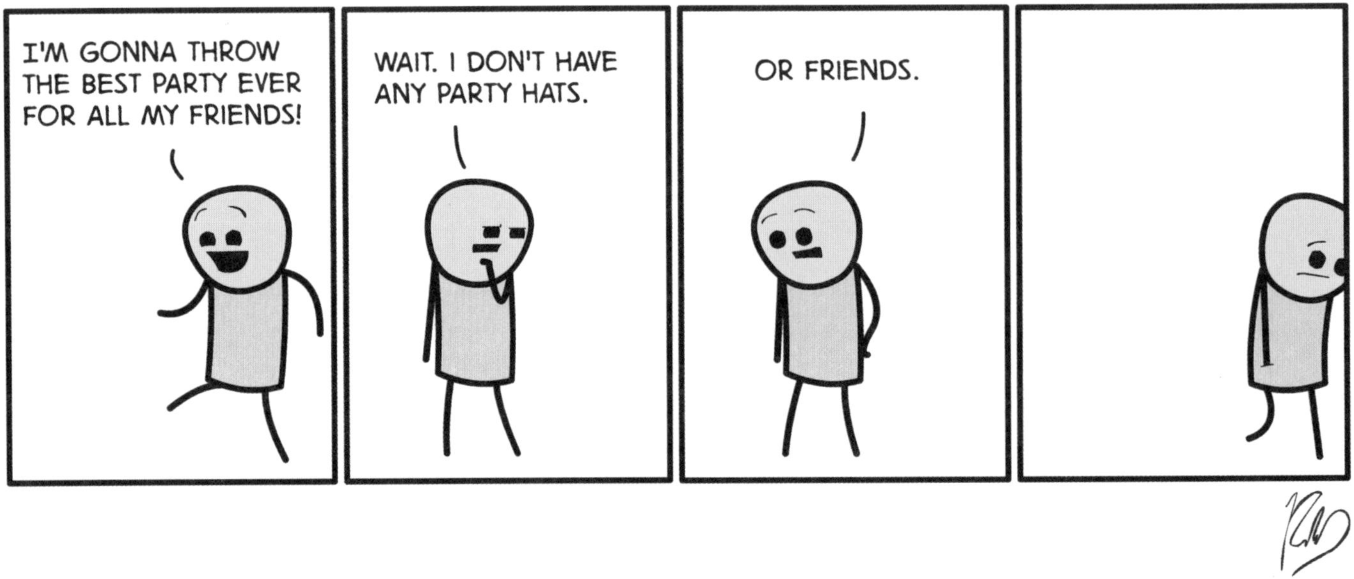
I'M GONNA THROW THE BEST PARTY EVER FOR ALL MY FRIENDS!
WAIT. I DON'T HAVE ANY PARTY HATS.
OR FRIENDS.

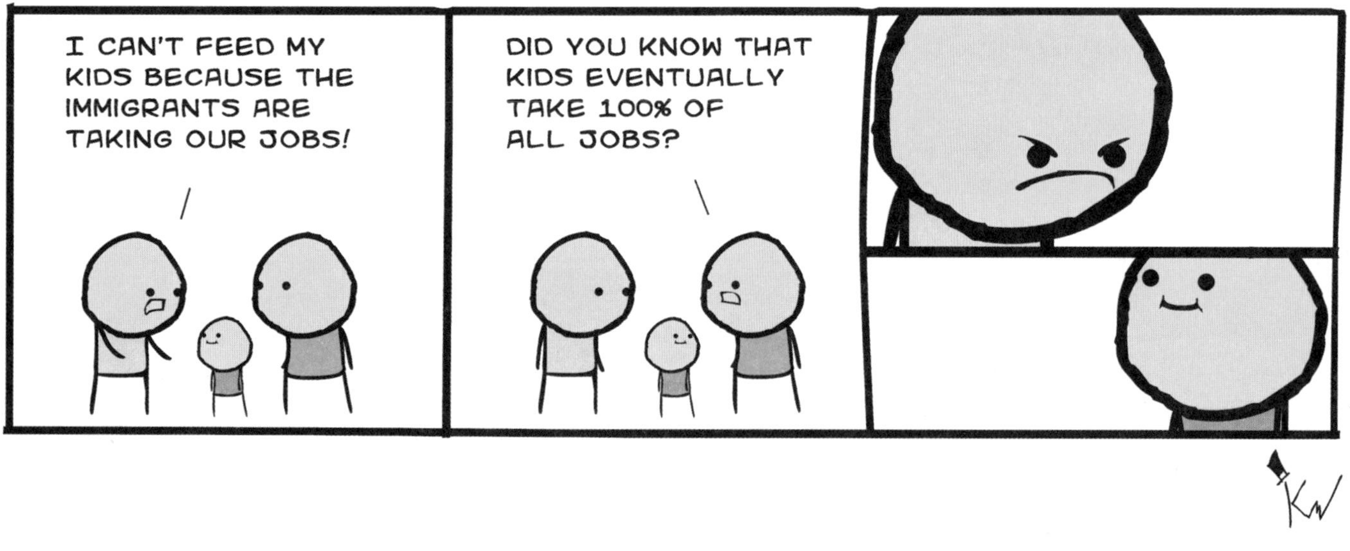
I CAN'T FEED MY KIDS BECAUSE THE IMMIGRANTS ARE TAKING OUR JOBS!
DID YOU KNOW THAT KIDS EVENTUALLY TAKE 100% OF ALL JOBS?

HEY, WANNA GO GET SOME DRINKS?
WHO'S GOING?
JUST YOU AND ME.
NAH, I HATE THOSE GUYS.

YOU ARE A WHITE MAN, AND THAT IS FUCKED UP.
HEY WHOA, THIS HAS NOTHING TO DO WITH MY RACIAL MAKEUP
THIS HAS EVERYTHING TO DO WITH THAT.

I THOUGHT YOU QUIT DRINKING LAST WEEK.
I SAVED MY PROGRESS.

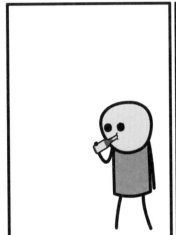

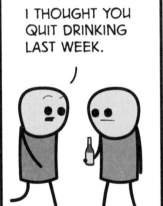

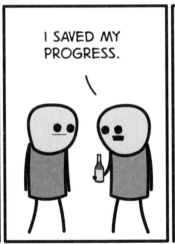

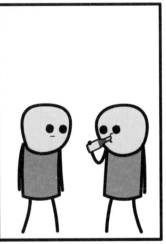

DAD, I CAN'T SLEEP. A MONSTER KEEPS COMING INTO MY ROOM AT NIGHT.
IF YOU CLOSE YOUR EYES AND STOP BELIEVING IN HIM, HE'LL VANISH!
POOF

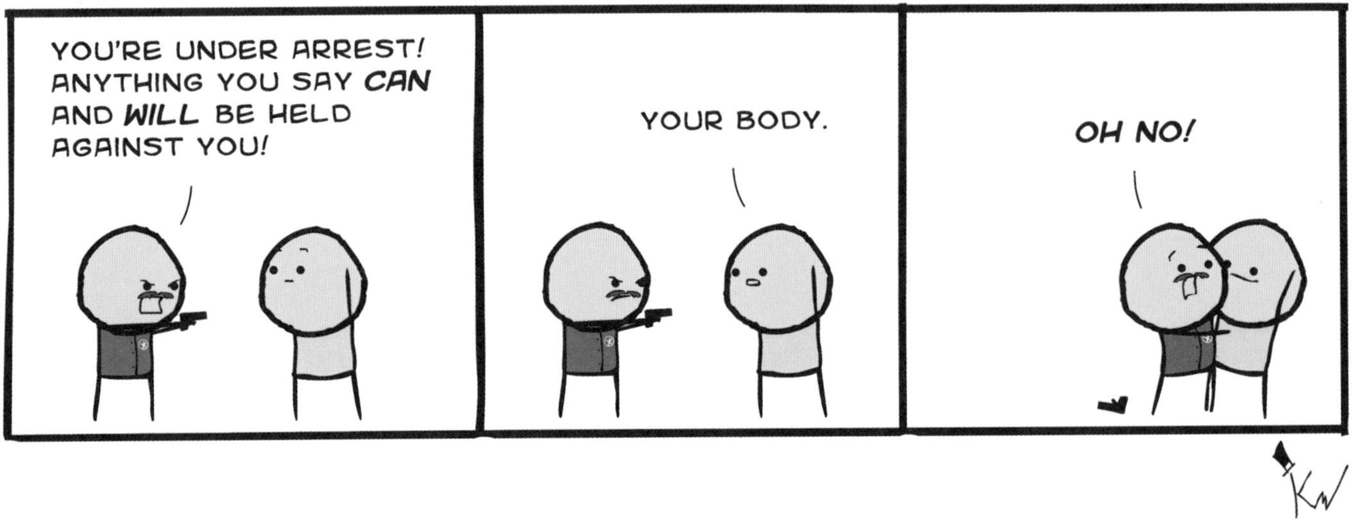
YOU'RE UNDER ARREST! ANYTHING YOU SAY CAN AND WILL BE HELD AGAINST YOU!
YOUR BODY.
OH NO!
KW

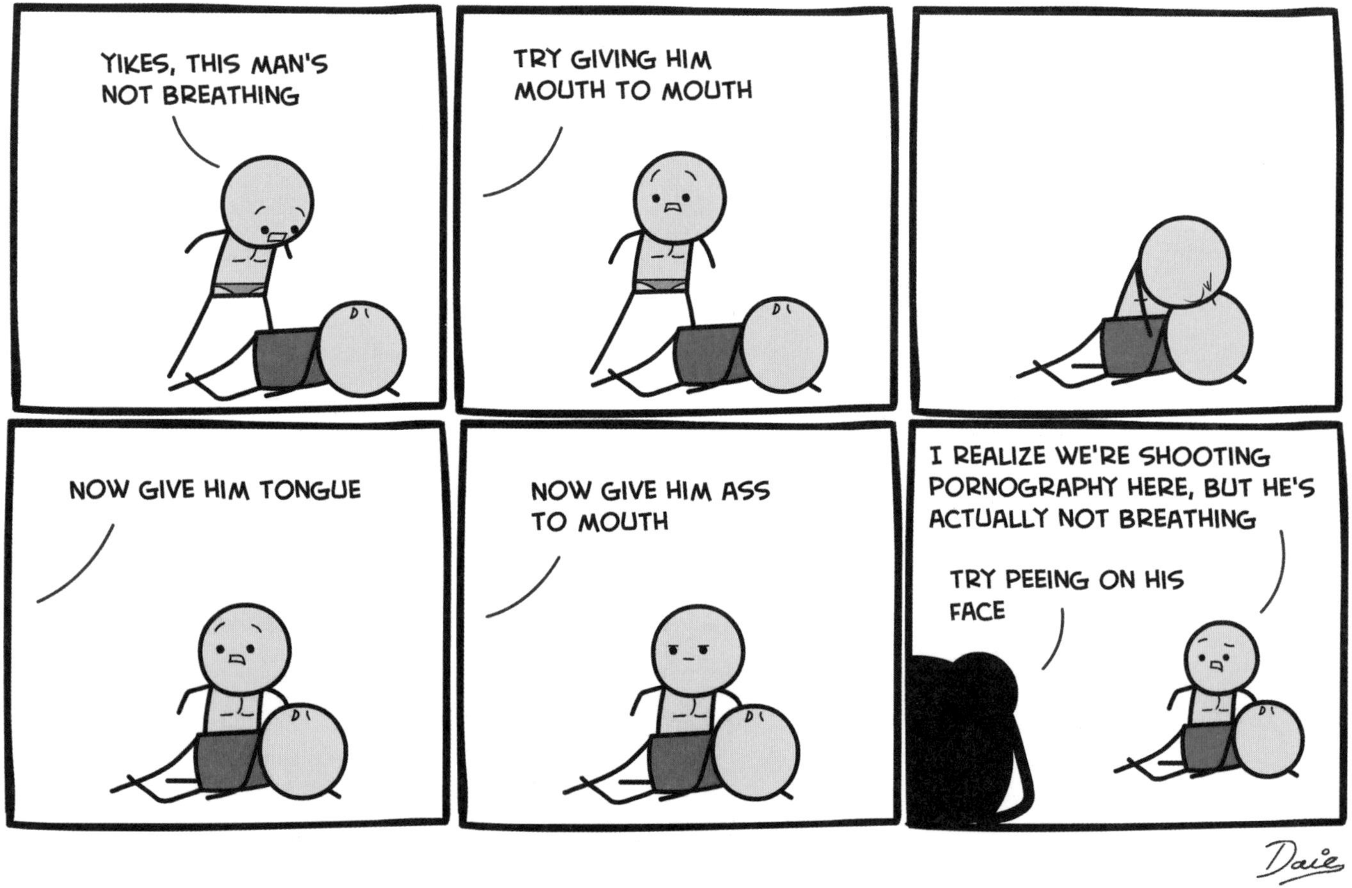
YIKES, THIS MAN'S NOT BREATHING
TRY GIVING HIM MOUTH TO MOUTH
NOW GIVE HIM TONGUE
NOW GIVE HIM ASS TO MOUTH
I REALIZE WE'RE SHOOTING PORNOGRAPHY HERE, BUT HE'S ACTUALLY NOT BREATHING
TRY PEEING ON HIS FACE
Dave

I'M HERE FOR YOU, TED.
NO, **NO!** I'M NOT READY TO GO YET! I **WON'T GO!**
NO NO, I THINK YOU'RE MISUNDERSTANDING ME. WHAT I MEAN IS I'M HERE FOR YOU **AS A FRIEND.**
AWWWW, THATS SO NICE OF YOU, DEATH!
FRIEND HUG!
GETS EM EVERY TIME
Dale

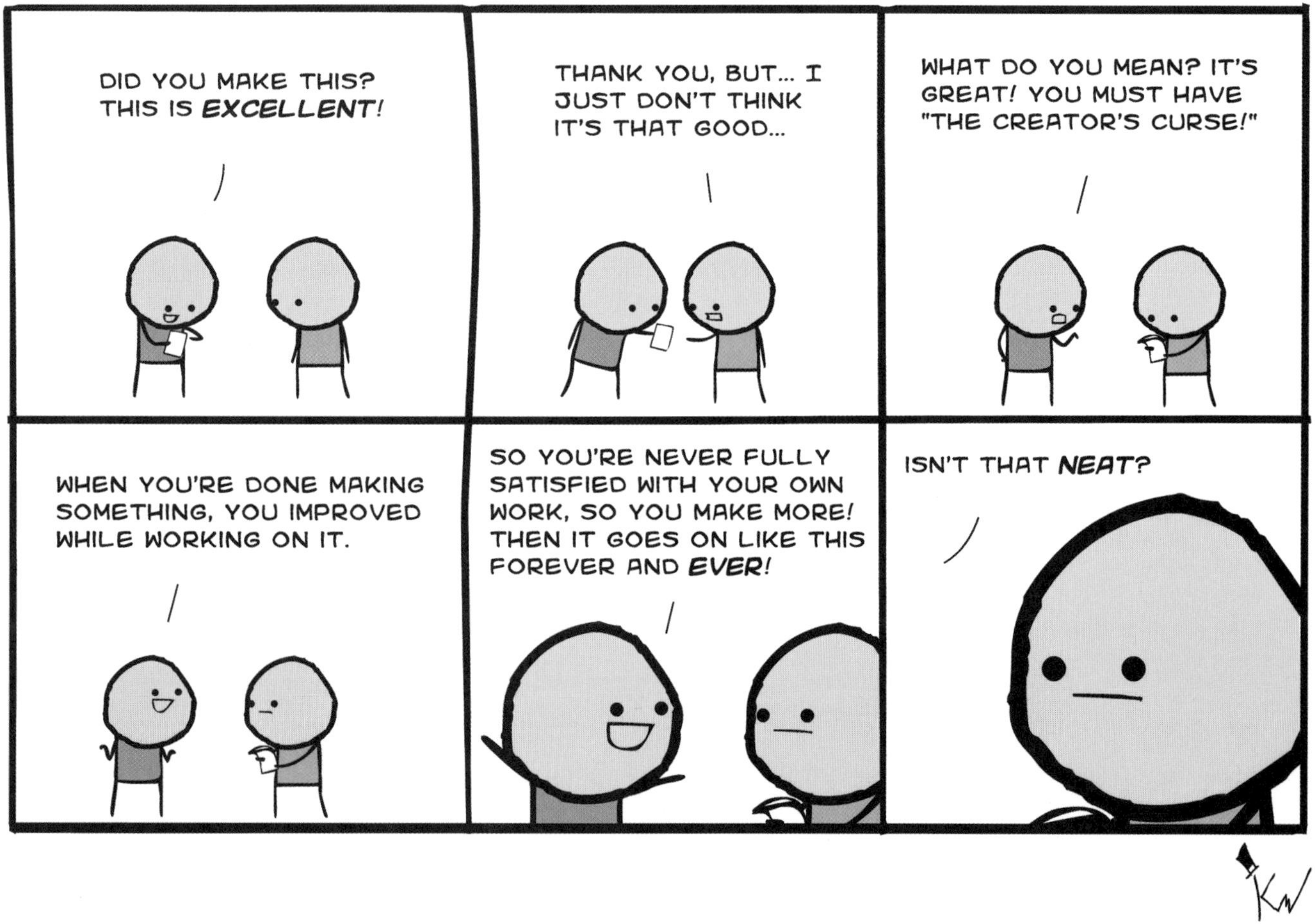
DID YOU MAKE THIS? THIS IS EXCELLENT!
THANK YOU, BUT... I JUST DON'T THINK IT'S THAT GOOD...
WHAT DO YOU MEAN? IT'S GREAT! YOU MUST HAVE "THE CREATOR'S CURSE!"
WHEN YOU'RE DONE MAKING SOMETHING, YOU IMPROVED WHILE WORKING ON IT.
SO YOU'RE NEVER FULLY SATISFIED WITH YOUR OWN WORK, SO YOU MAKE MORE! THEN IT GOES ON LIKE THIS FOREVER AND EVER!
ISN'T THAT NEAT?
KW

MAN, I AM **LITERALLY** STARVING.
ACTUALLY, YOU'RE MISUSING THE TERM 'LITERALLY'. WHAT YOU MEAN IS THAT YOU'RE FIGURATIVELY-

HELLO THERE, I'M A RACIST!
THAT'S HORRIBLE. WHY WOULD YOU EVEN ADMIT SOMETHING LIKE THAT?
HAHA, NO, I'M A RACIST AS IN I LOVE RUNNING AND RACING PEOPLE!
OOOH, HAHA
NOT BLACK PEOPLE THOUGH, THEY CAN ALL RUN FASTER
Dave

HEY, BUDDY! LONG TIME NO SEE! HOW HAVE YOU BEEN?
NOT SO GOOD... I'VE KINDA BEEN THINKING ABOUT KILLING MYSELF...
COME ON, MAN... DON'T SAY THAT. THINK ABOUT YOUR FRIENDS AND FAMILY.
WHAT IF THEY WANT TO BE THE ONE TO KILL YOU?

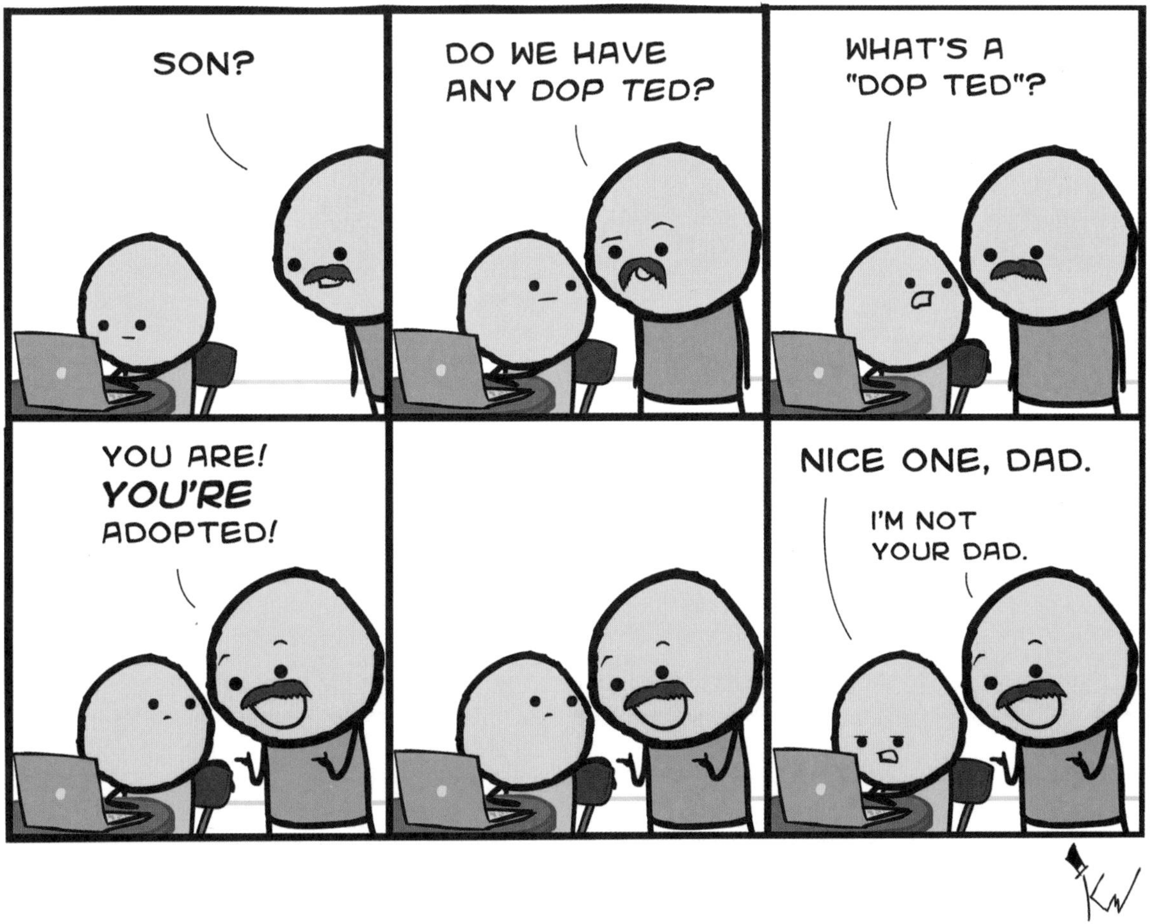
SON?
DO WE HAVE ANY DOP TED?
WHAT'S A "DOP TED"?
YOU ARE! *YOU'RE* ADOPTED!
NICE ONE, DAD.
I'M NOT YOUR DAD.
KW

WHAT I THINK YOU HAVE IS AN ATTITUDE PROBLEM. TRY TO THINK ON THE POSITIVE SIDE OF THINGS!
I'M DYING SLOWLY.
THINK OF IT AS LIVING QUICKLY!

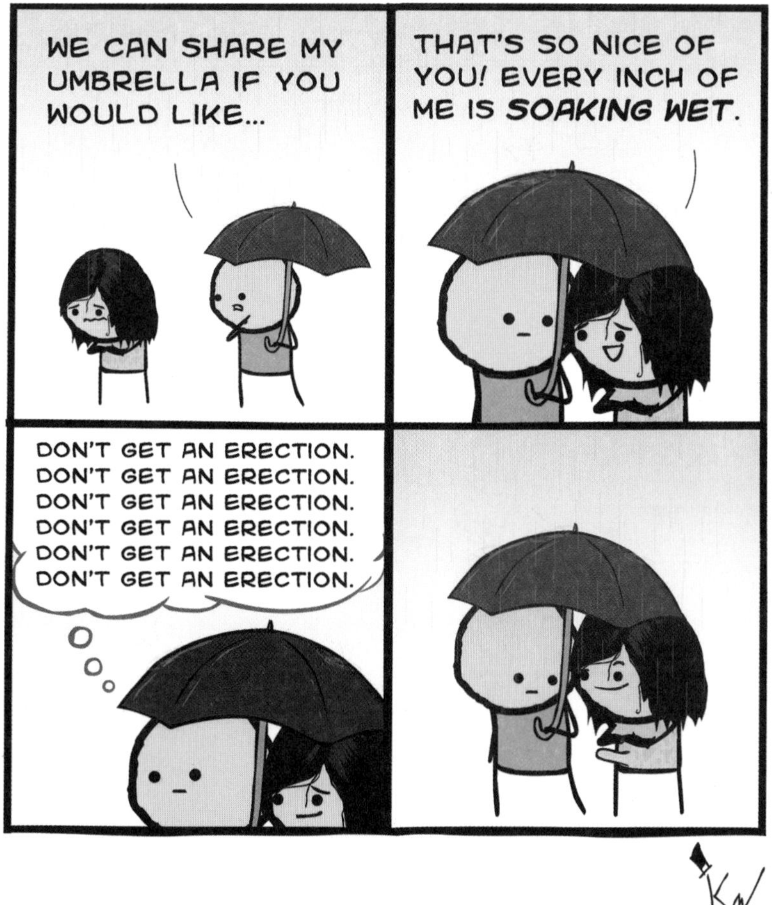
WE CAN SHARE MY UMBRELLA IF YOU WOULD LIKE...
THAT'S SO NICE OF YOU! EVERY INCH OF ME IS SOAKING WET.
DON'T GET AN ERECTION. DON'T GET AN ERECTION. DON'T GET AN ERECTION. DON'T GET AN ERECTION. DON'T GET AN ERECTION. DON'T GET AN ERECTION.

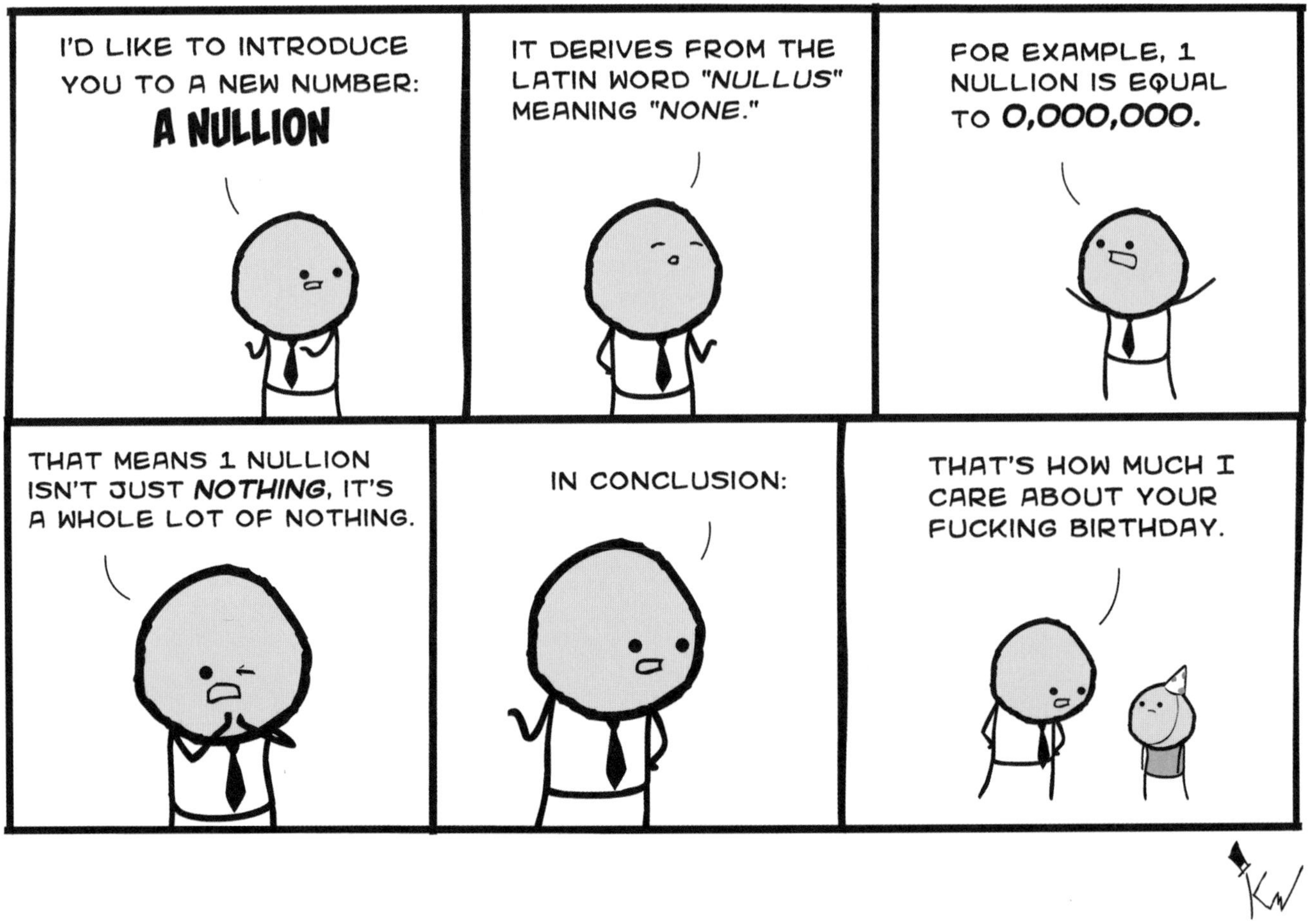
I'D LIKE TO INTRODUCE YOU TO A NEW NUMBER:
A NULLION
IT DERIVES FROM THE LATIN WORD "NULLUS" MEANING "NONE."
FOR EXAMPLE, 1 NULLION IS EQUAL TO 0,000,000.
THAT MEANS 1 NULLION ISN'T JUST NOTHING, IT'S A WHOLE LOT OF NOTHING.
IN CONCLUSION:
THAT'S HOW MUCH I CARE ABOUT YOUR FUCKING BIRTHDAY.

CONGRATULATIONS! IT'S A BABY BOY!
WAIT... THIS BABY LOOKS NOTHING LIKE ME!
MIKE, YOU SON OF A BITCH!!

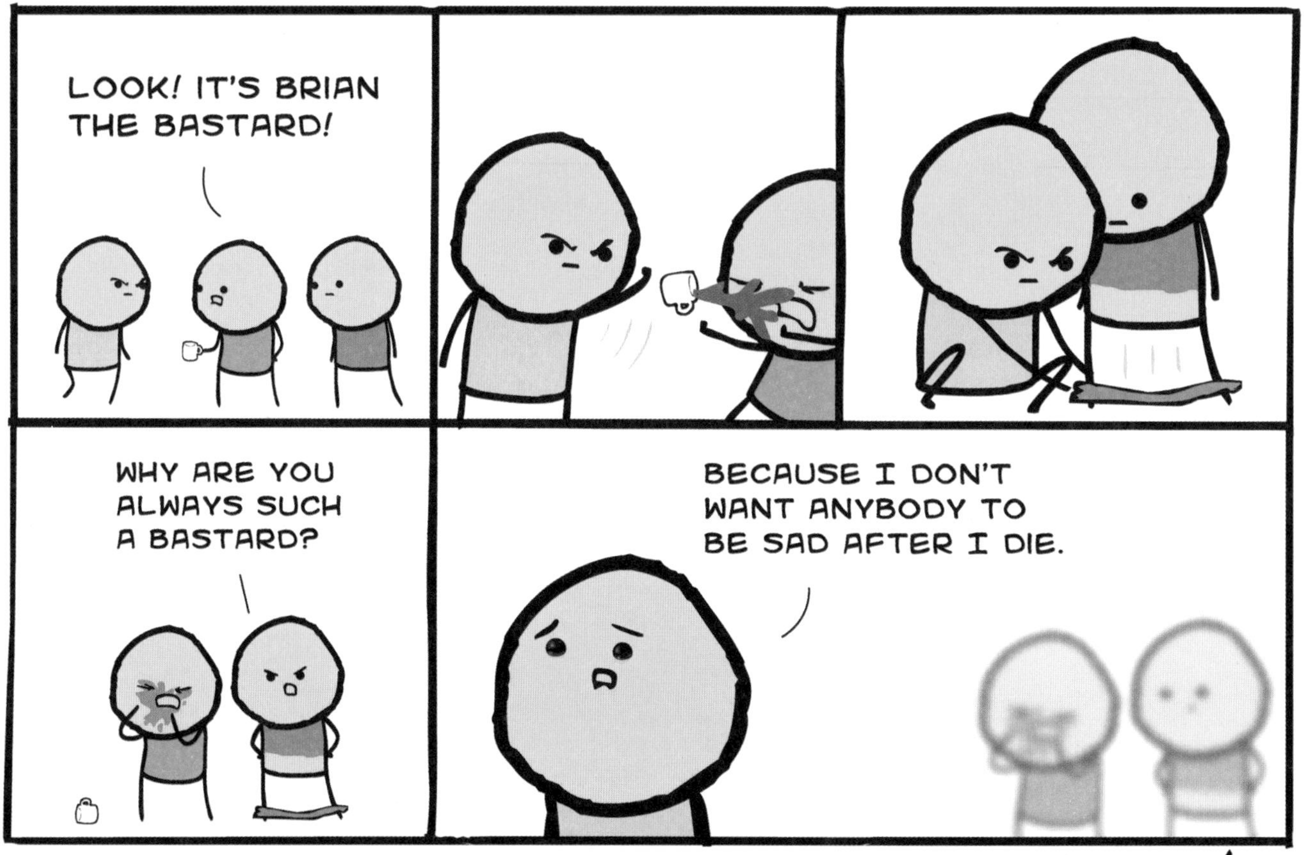
LOOK! IT'S BRIAN THE BASTARD!
WHY ARE YOU ALWAYS SUCH A BASTARD?
BECAUSE I DON'T WANT ANYBODY TO BE SAD AFTER I DIE.

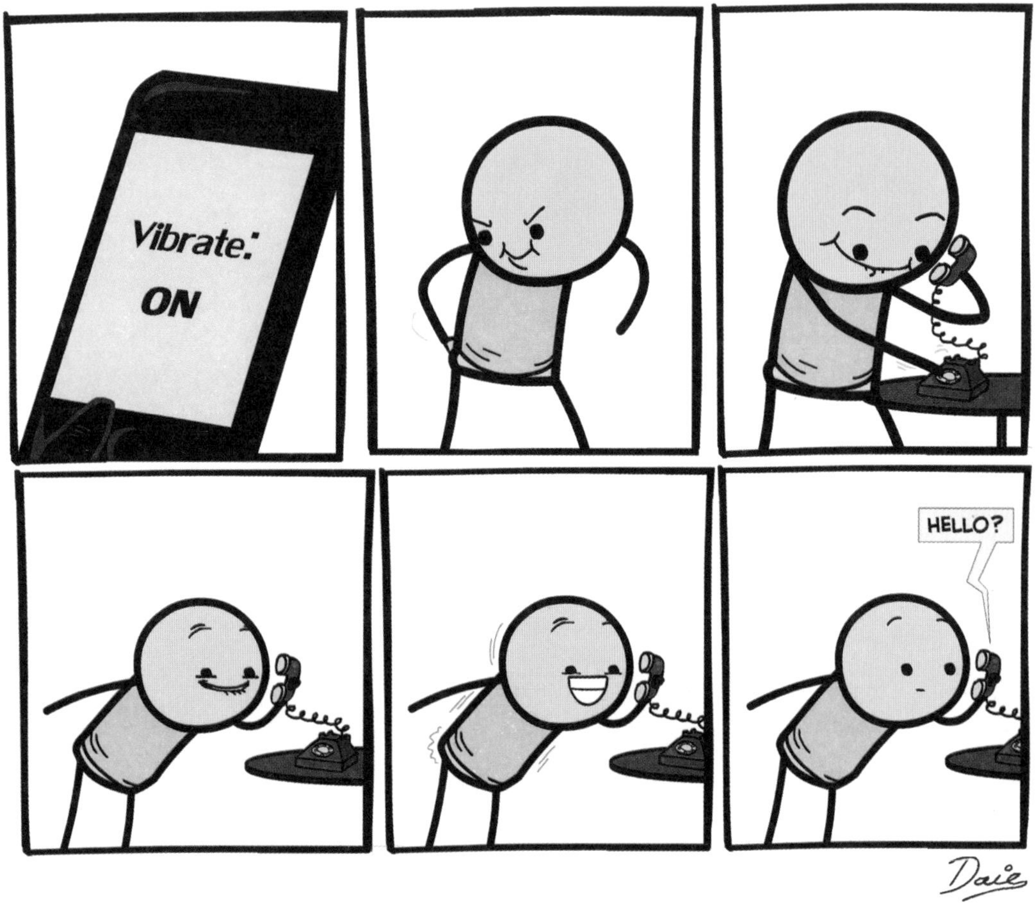
Vibrate:
ON
HELLO?
Dave

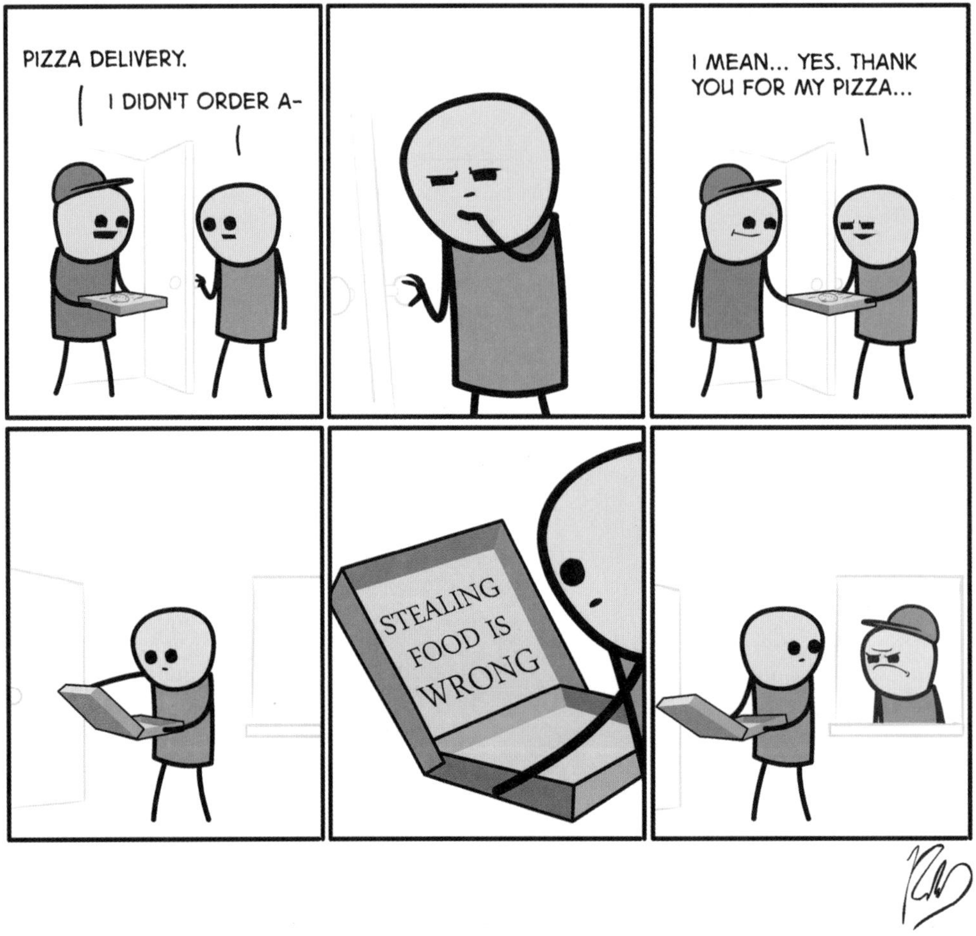
PIZZA DELIVERY.
I DIDN'T ORDER A-
I MEAN... YES. THANK YOU FOR MY PIZZA...
STEALING FOOD IS WRONG

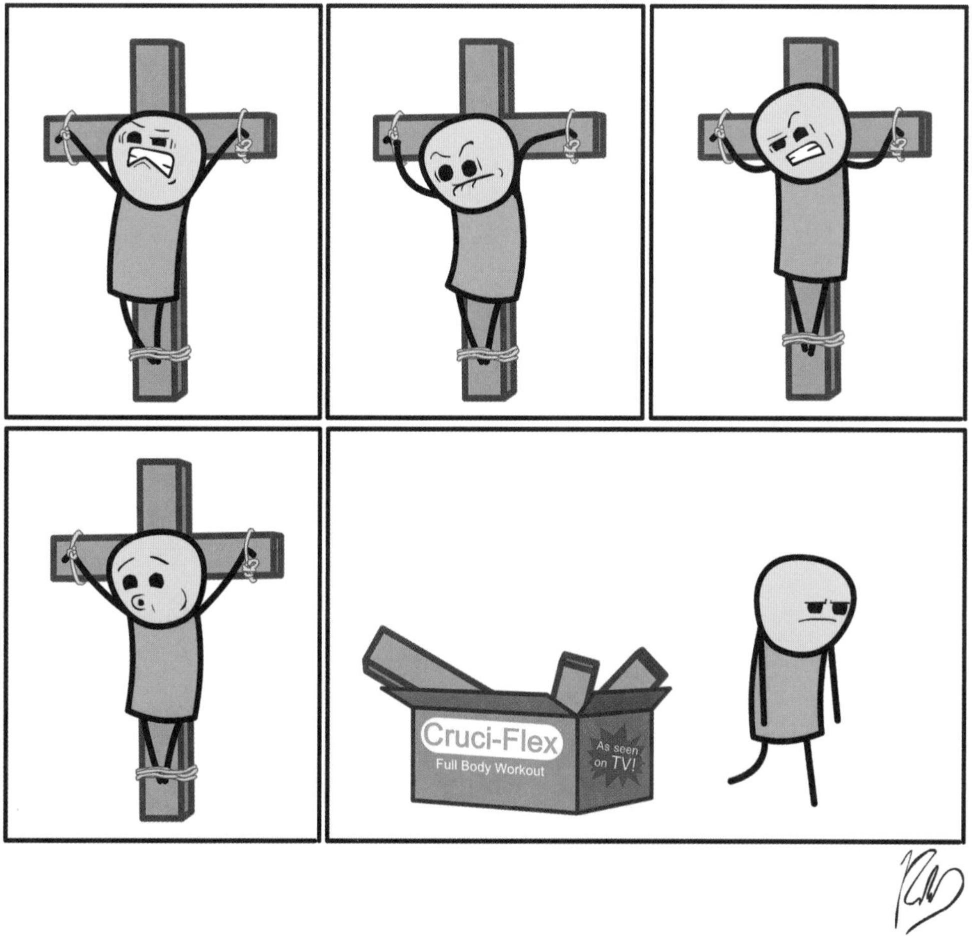
Cruci-Flex
Full Body Workout
As seen on TV!

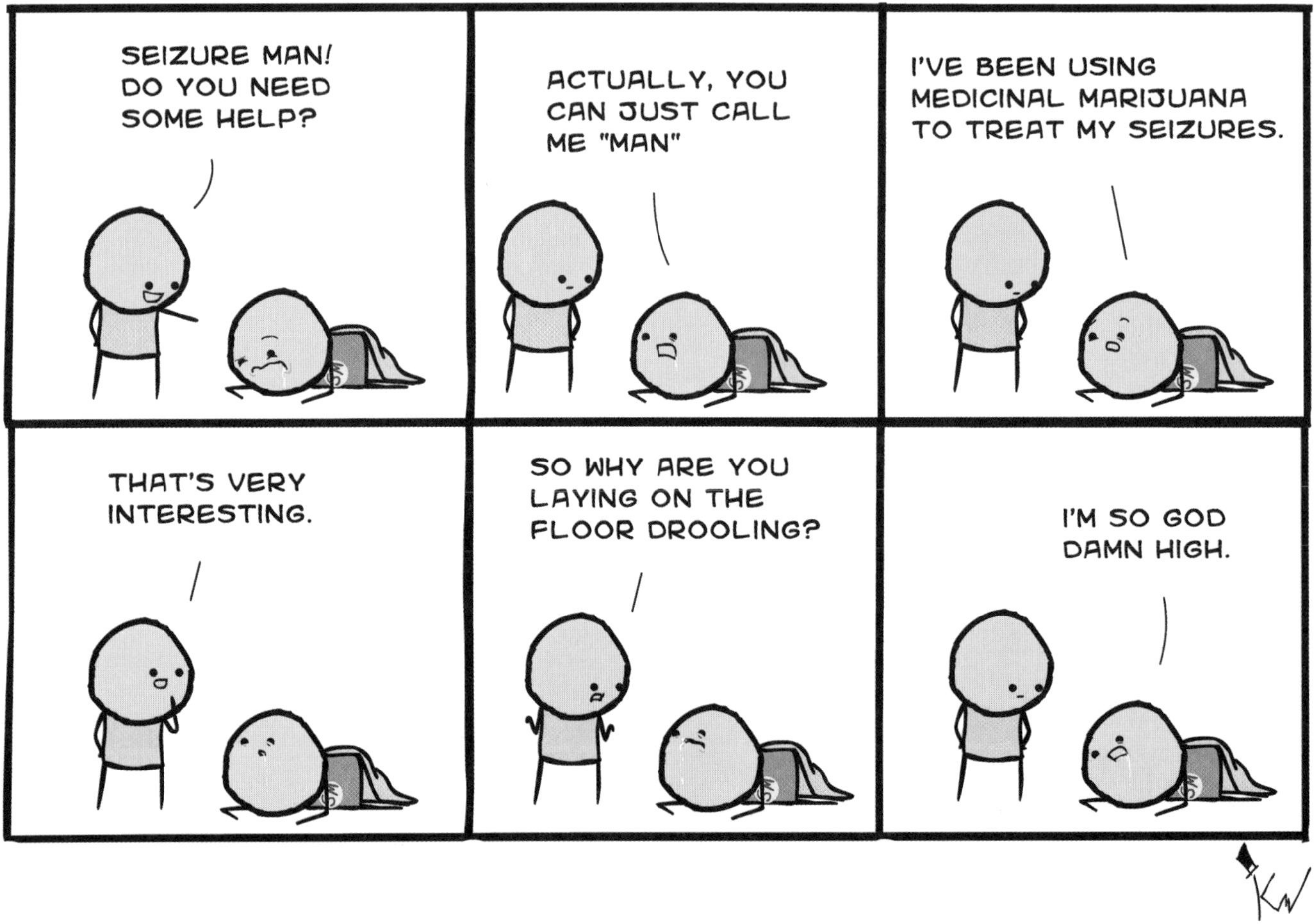
SEIZURE MAN! DO YOU NEED SOME HELP?
ACTUALLY, YOU CAN JUST CALL ME "MAN"
I'VE BEEN USING MEDICINAL MARIJUANA TO TREAT MY SEIZURES.
THAT'S VERY INTERESTING.
SO WHY ARE YOU LAYING ON THE FLOOR DROOLING?
I'M SO GOD DAMN HIGH.

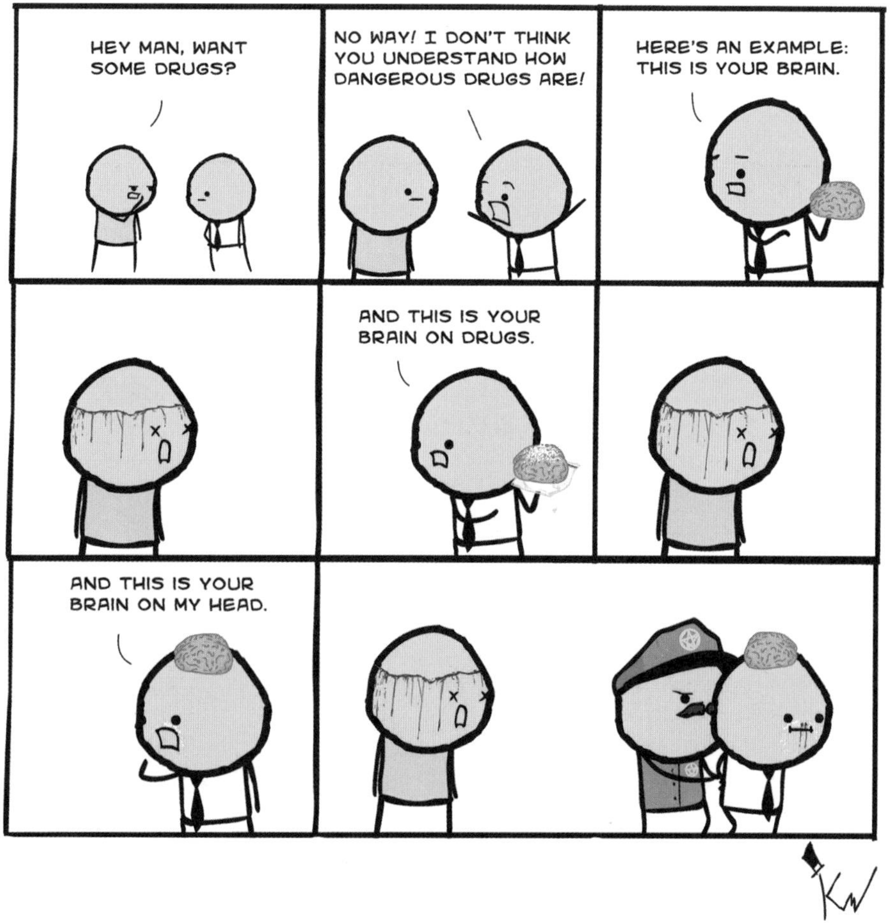
HEY MAN, WANT SOME DRUGS?
NO WAY! I DON'T THINK YOU UNDERSTAND HOW DANGEROUS DRUGS ARE!
HERE'S AN EXAMPLE: THIS IS YOUR BRAIN.
AND THIS IS YOUR BRAIN ON DRUGS.
AND THIS IS YOUR BRAIN ON MY HEAD.

HEY, CHECK OUT MY COOL NEW SMARTPHONE!
OH YEAH? WELL CHECK OUT MY COOL NEW MEGAPHONE!
SHUT THE FUCK UP ABOUT YOUR NEW PHONE.
Dave

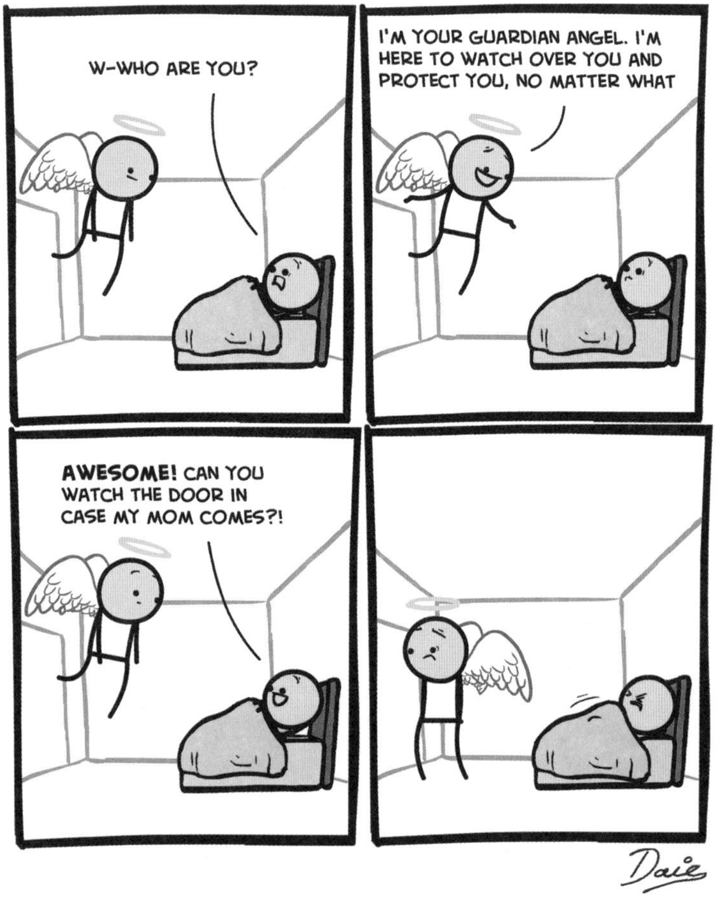
W-WHO ARE YOU?
I'M YOUR GUARDIAN ANGEL. I'M HERE TO WATCH OVER YOU AND PROTECT YOU, NO MATTER WHAT
AWESOME! CAN YOU WATCH THE DOOR IN CASE MY MOM COMES?!
Dave

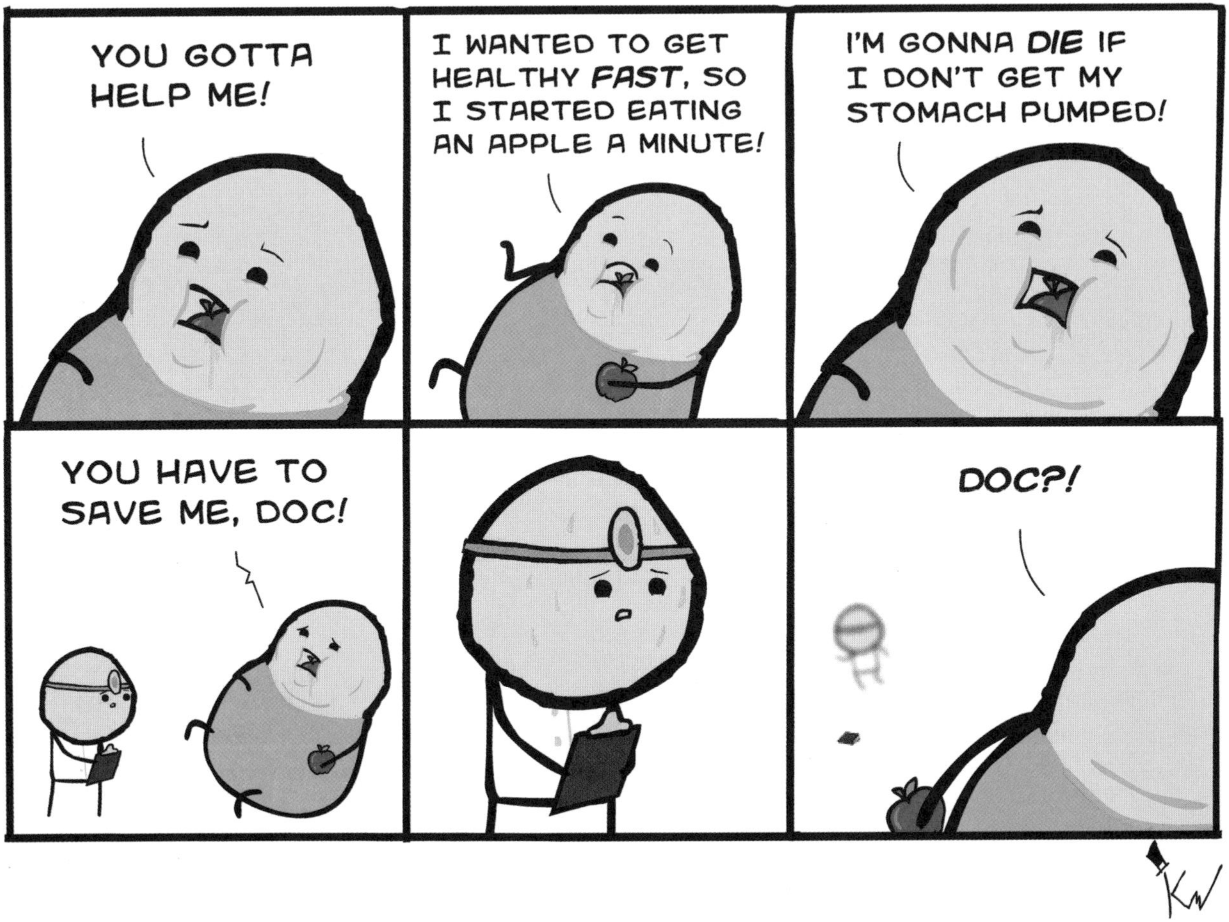
YOU GOTTA HELP ME!
I WANTED TO GET HEALTHY FAST, SO I STARTED EATING AN APPLE A MINUTE!
I'M GONNA DIE IF I DON'T GET MY STOMACH PUMPED!
YOU HAVE TO SAVE ME, DOC!
DOC?!
KW

UGH, I LOST MY KEYS AGAIN.
WHY DO I KEEP LOSING STUFF ALL THE TIME?
MAYBE YOU'RE A MAGICIAN BUT DON'T REALIZE IT.

HEY, LOOK AT MY APPS
WHOA, THAT'S YOUR ASS, I THOUGHT YOU SAID APPS
WAY TO MAKE FUN OF MY SPEECH PROBLEM, APPSHOLE
Dave

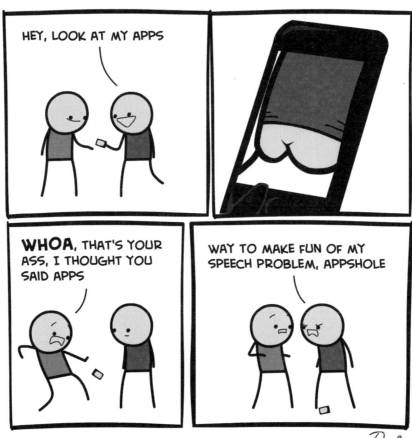

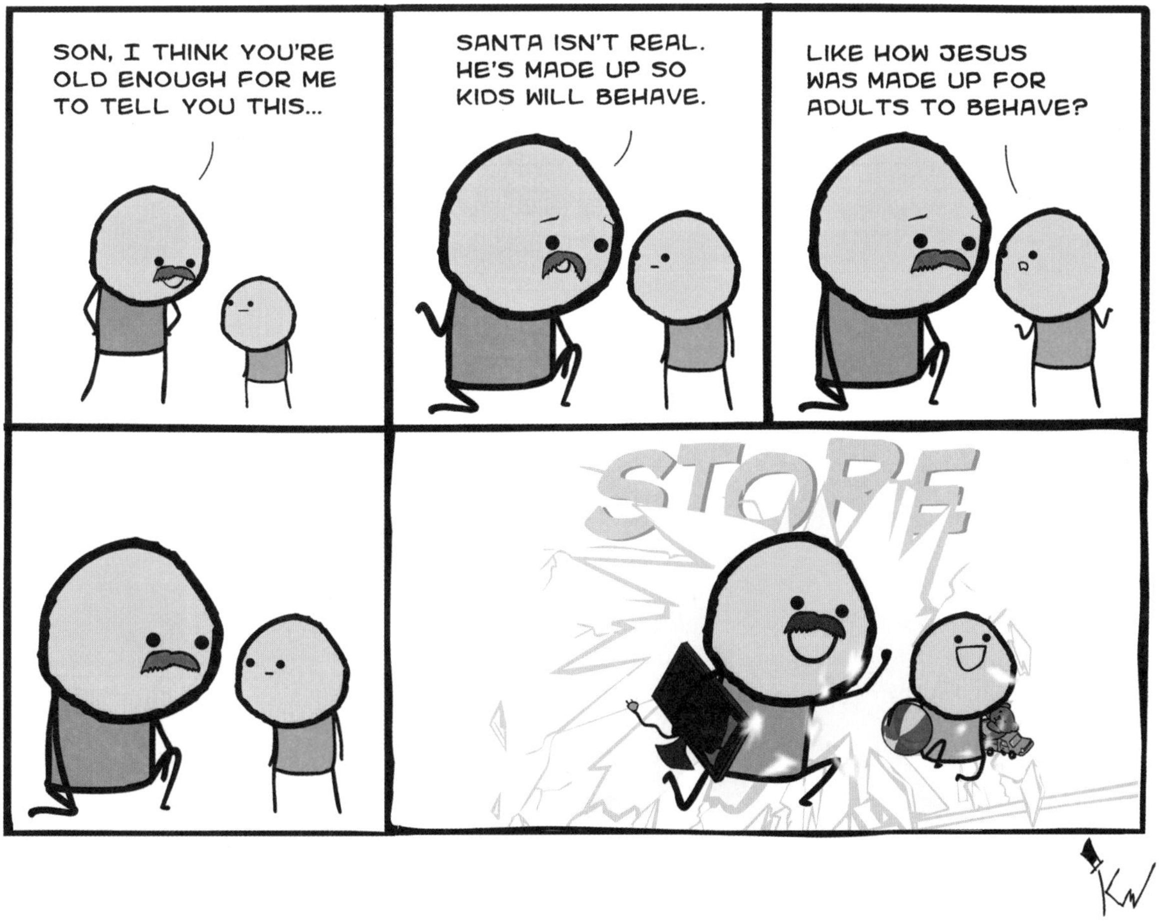
SON, I THINK YOU'RE OLD ENOUGH FOR ME TO TELL YOU THIS...
SANTA ISN'T REAL. HE'S MADE UP SO KIDS WILL BEHAVE.
LIKE HOW JESUS WAS MADE UP FOR ADULTS TO BEHAVE?
STORE

I DUNNO WHAT IT IS, I'VE JUST NEVER ENJOYED KALE.
HAVE YOU TRIED IT BAKED?
NO.

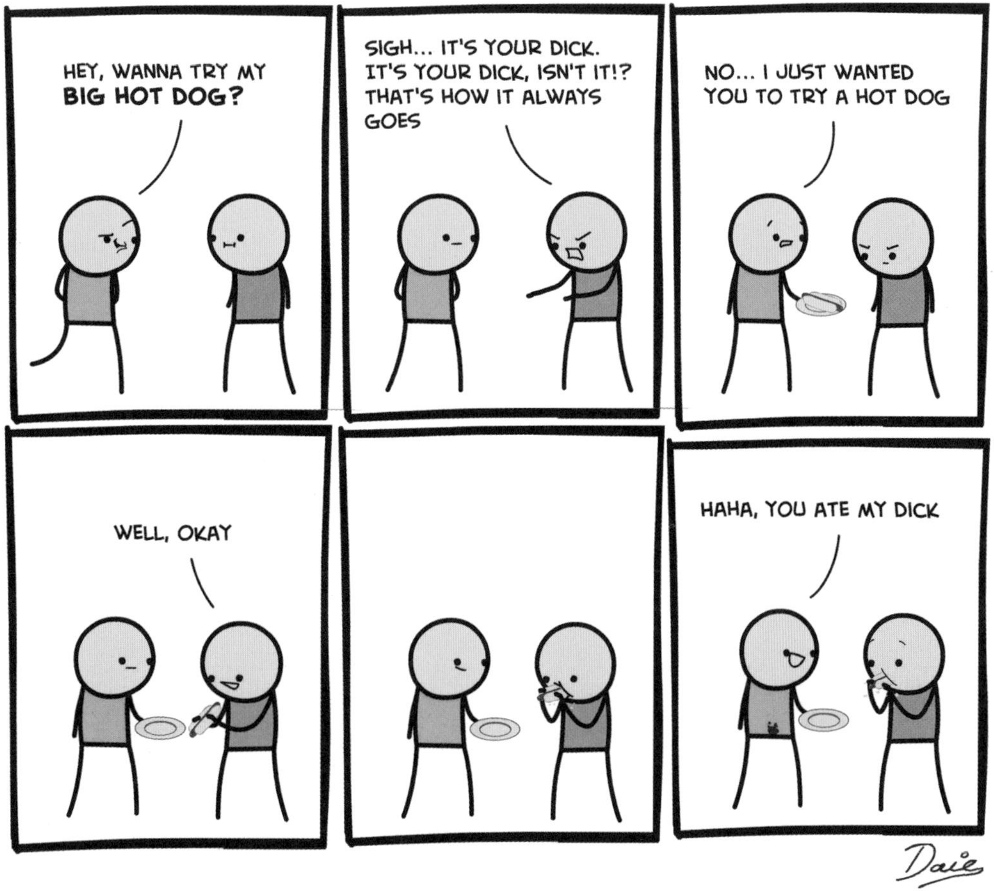
HEY, WANNA TRY MY **BIG HOT DOG?**
SIGH... IT'S YOUR DICK. IT'S YOUR DICK, ISN'T IT!? THAT'S HOW IT ALWAYS GOES
NO... I JUST WANTED YOU TO TRY A HOT DOG
WELL, OKAY
HAHA, YOU ATE MY DICK
Dave

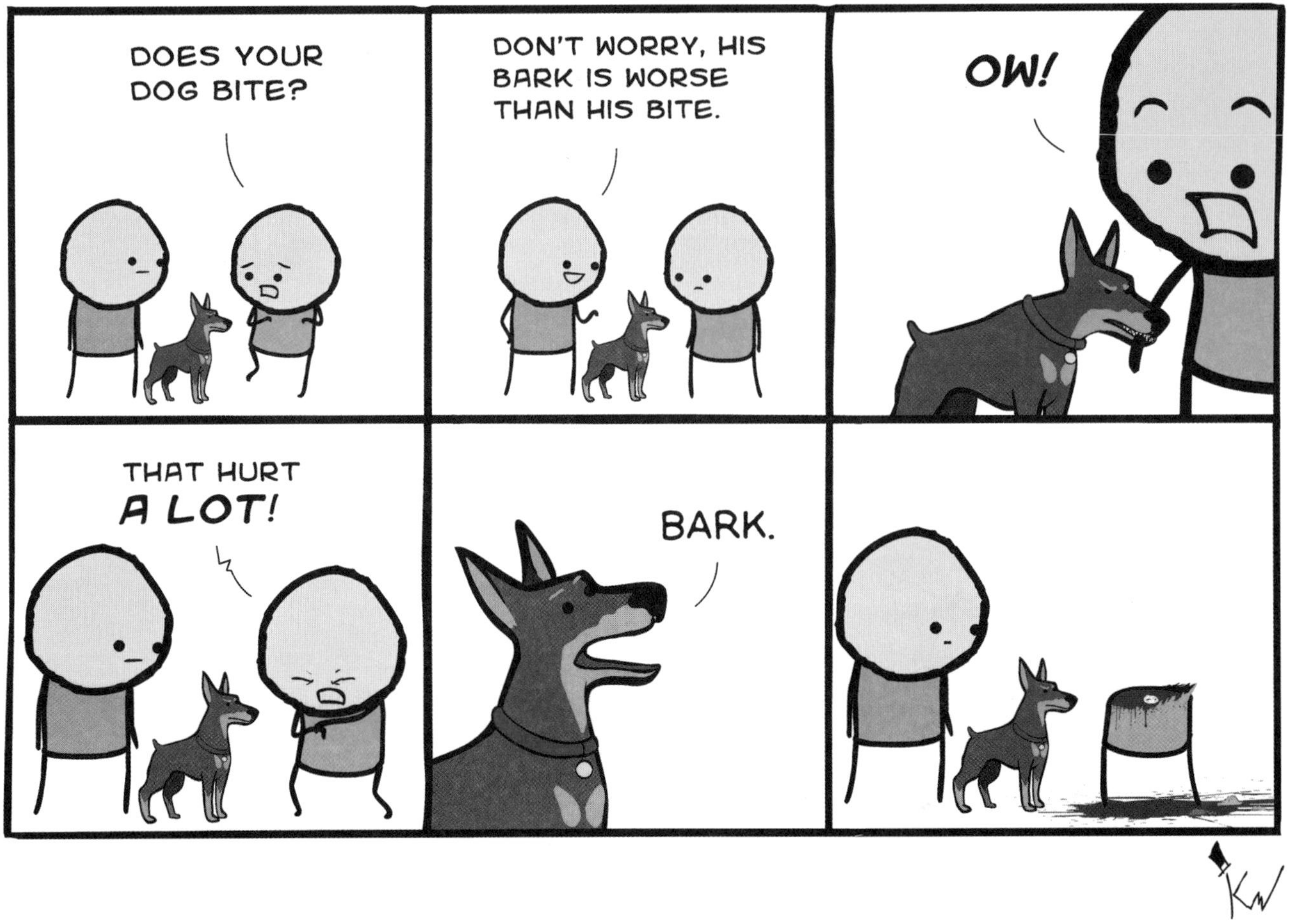
DOES YOUR DOG BITE?
DON'T WORRY, HIS BARK IS WORSE THAN HIS BITE.
OW!
THAT HURT A LOT!
BARK.

ARE YOU DOING MATH PROBLEMS FOR FUN?
YEAH. I LOVE BEING MENTALLY CHALLENGED.
WELL I'M GLAD YOU'VE COME TO TERMS WITH IT.
THANKS!

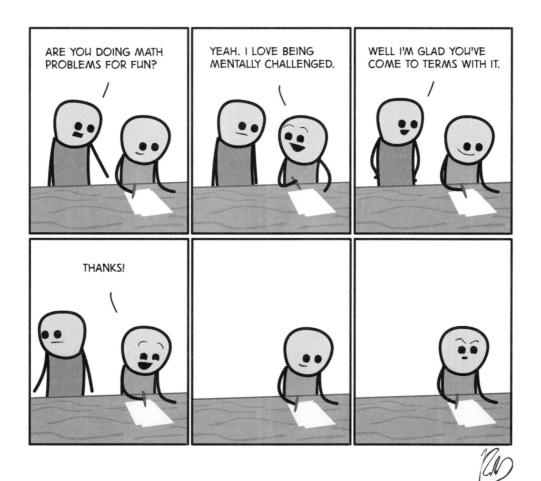

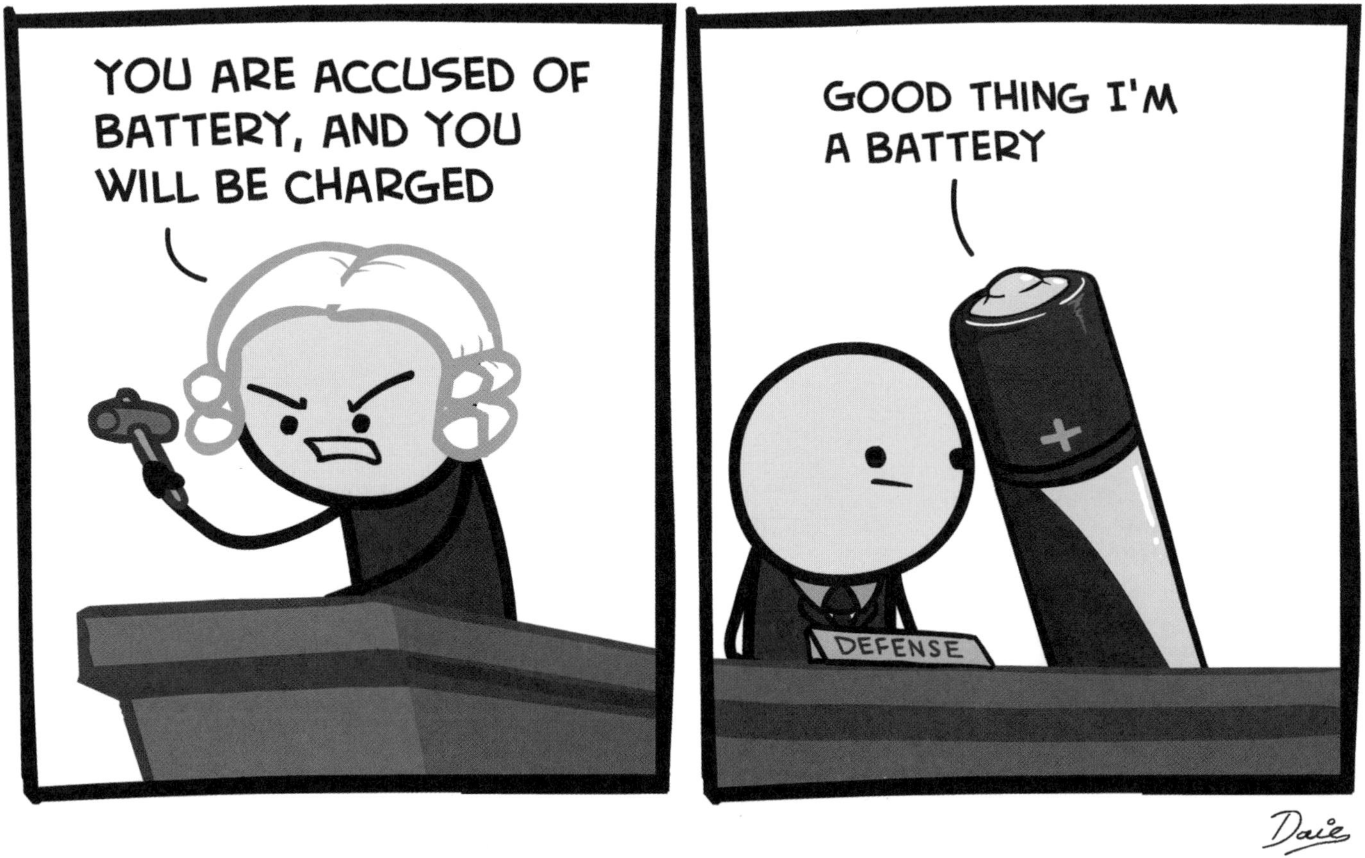
YOU ARE ACCUSED OF BATTERY, AND YOU WILL BE CHARGED
GOOD THING I'M A BATTERY
DEFENSE
Dale

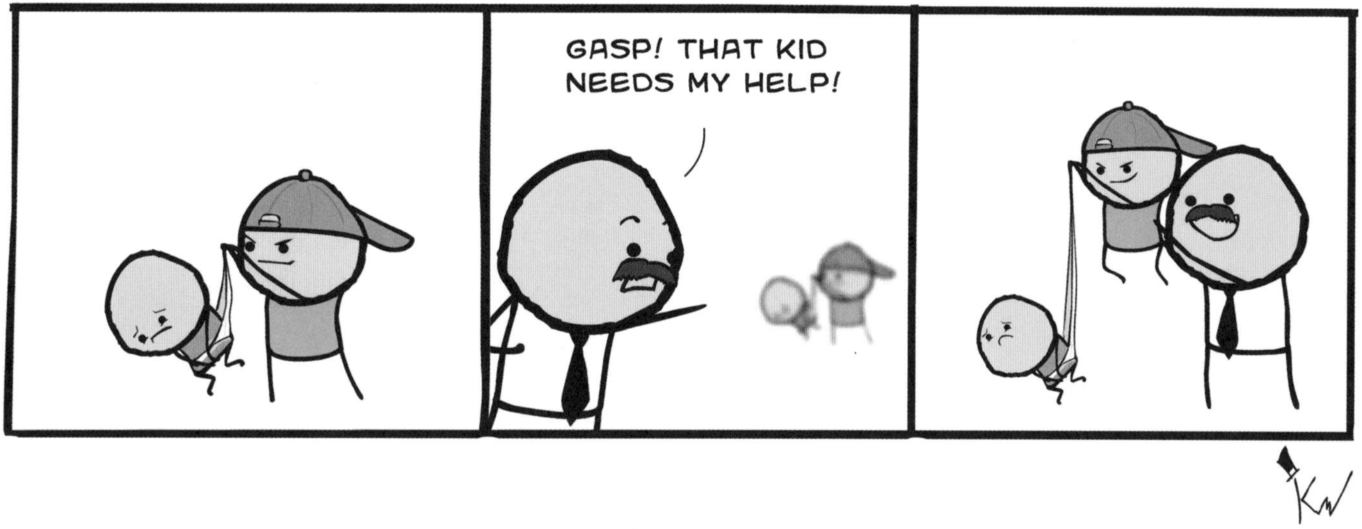
GASP! THAT KID NEEDS MY HELP!
KW

MY WIFE IS IN THAT BURNING BUILDING! PLEASE HELP ME, ***MIDDLE MAN!***
MM
THIS SOUNDS LIKE A JOB FOR THAT GUY!
MM
MM

OW, I BIT MY CHEEK!
OUCH, ARE YOU OKAY?
I THINK I ALSO BROKE MY SPINE
Dave

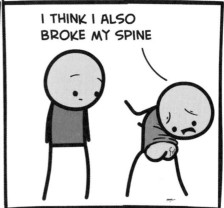

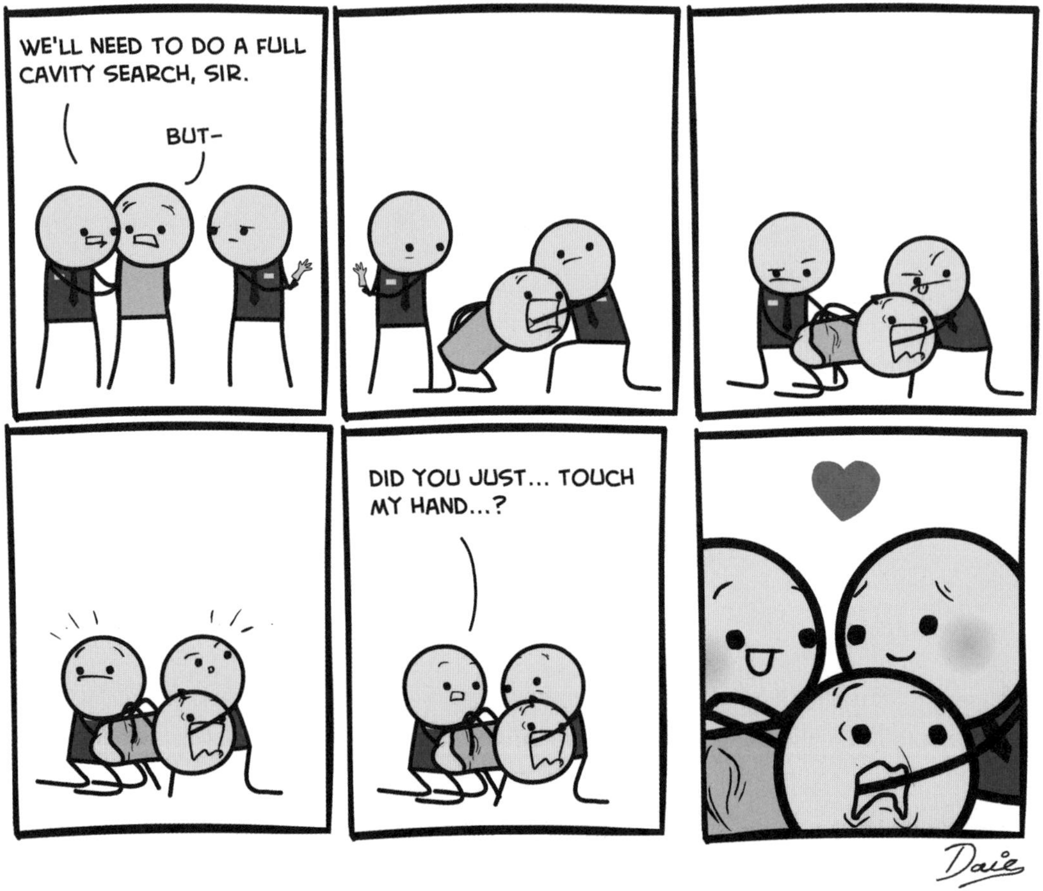
WE'LL NEED TO DO A FULL CAVITY SEARCH, SIR.
BUT-
DID YOU JUST... TOUCH MY HAND...?
Dave

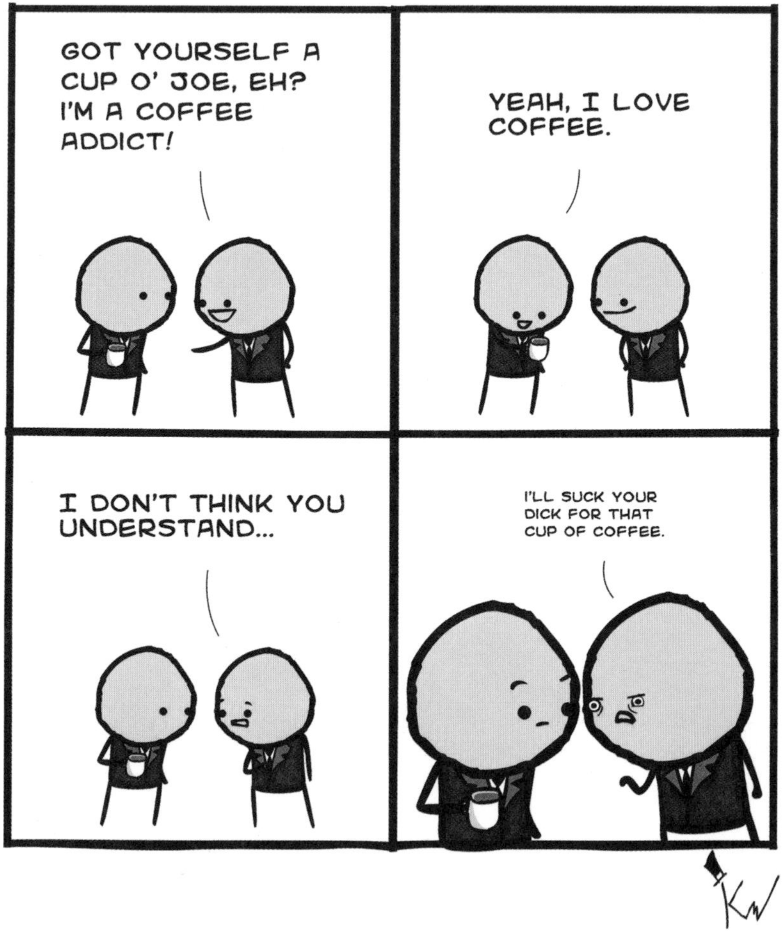
GOT YOURSELF A CUP O' JOE, EH? I'M A COFFEE ADDICT!
YEAH, I LOVE COFFEE.
I DON'T THINK YOU UNDERSTAND...
I'LL SUCK YOUR DICK FOR THAT CUP OF COFFEE.

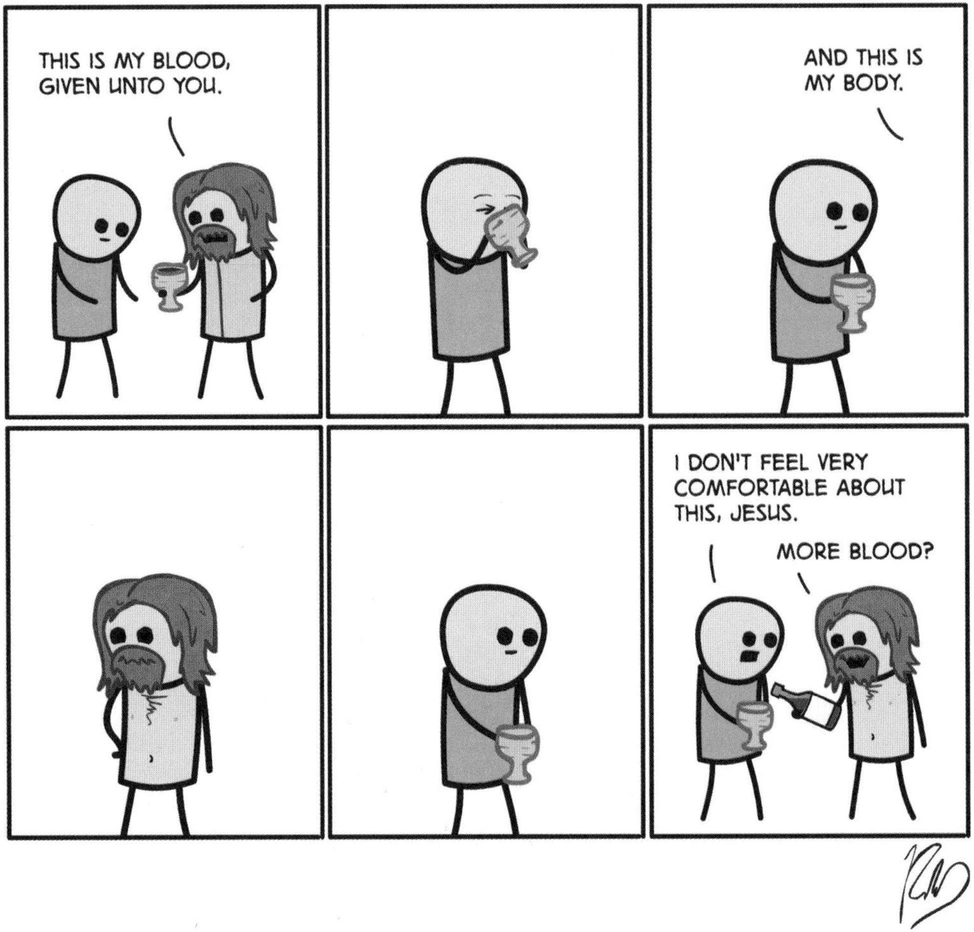
THIS IS MY BLOOD, GIVEN UNTO YOU.
AND THIS IS MY BODY.
I DON'T FEEL VERY COMFORTABLE ABOUT THIS, JESUS.
MORE BLOOD?

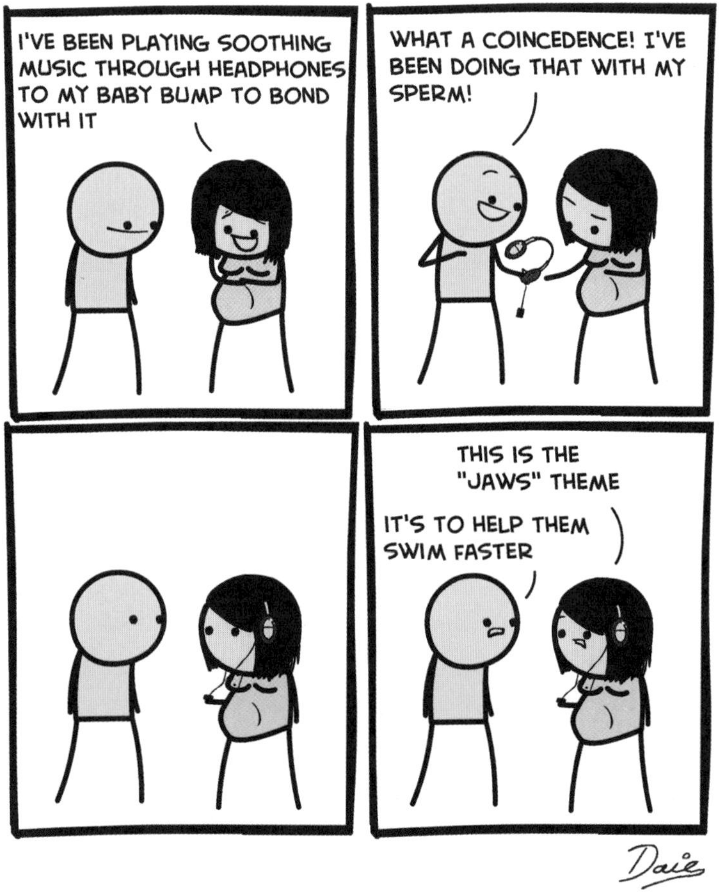
I'VE BEEN PLAYING SOOTHING MUSIC THROUGH HEADPHONES TO MY BABY BUMP TO BOND WITH IT
WHAT A COINCEDENCE! I'VE BEEN DOING THAT WITH MY SPERM!
THIS IS THE "JAWS" THEME
IT'S TO HELP THEM SWIM FASTER
Dave

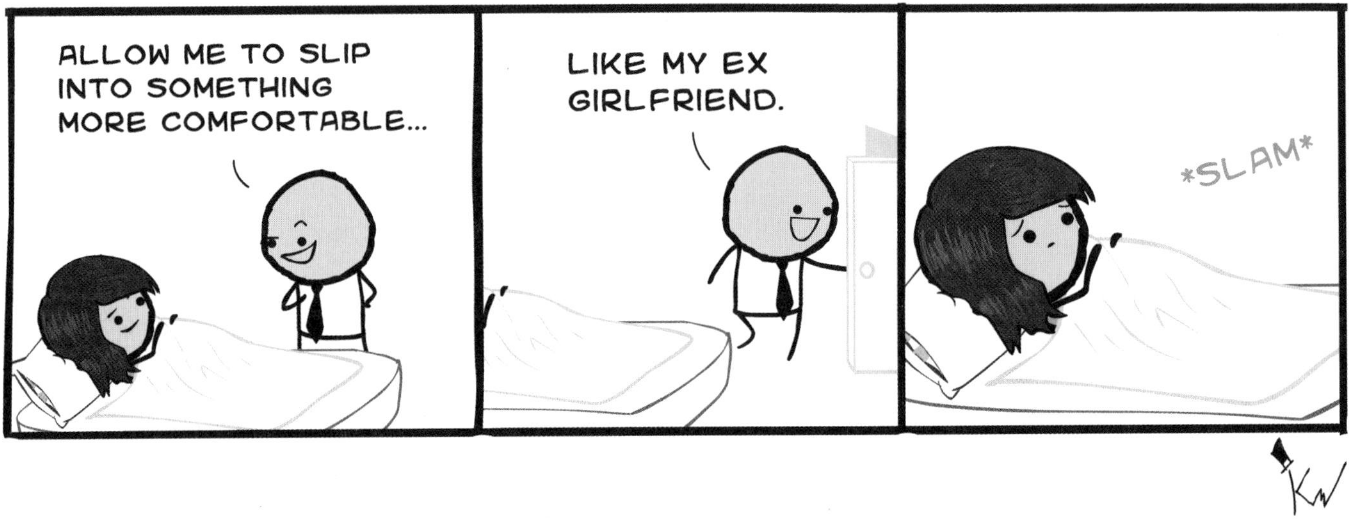
ALLOW ME TO SLIP INTO SOMETHING MORE COMFORTABLE...
LIKE MY EX GIRLFRIEND.
SLAM
KW

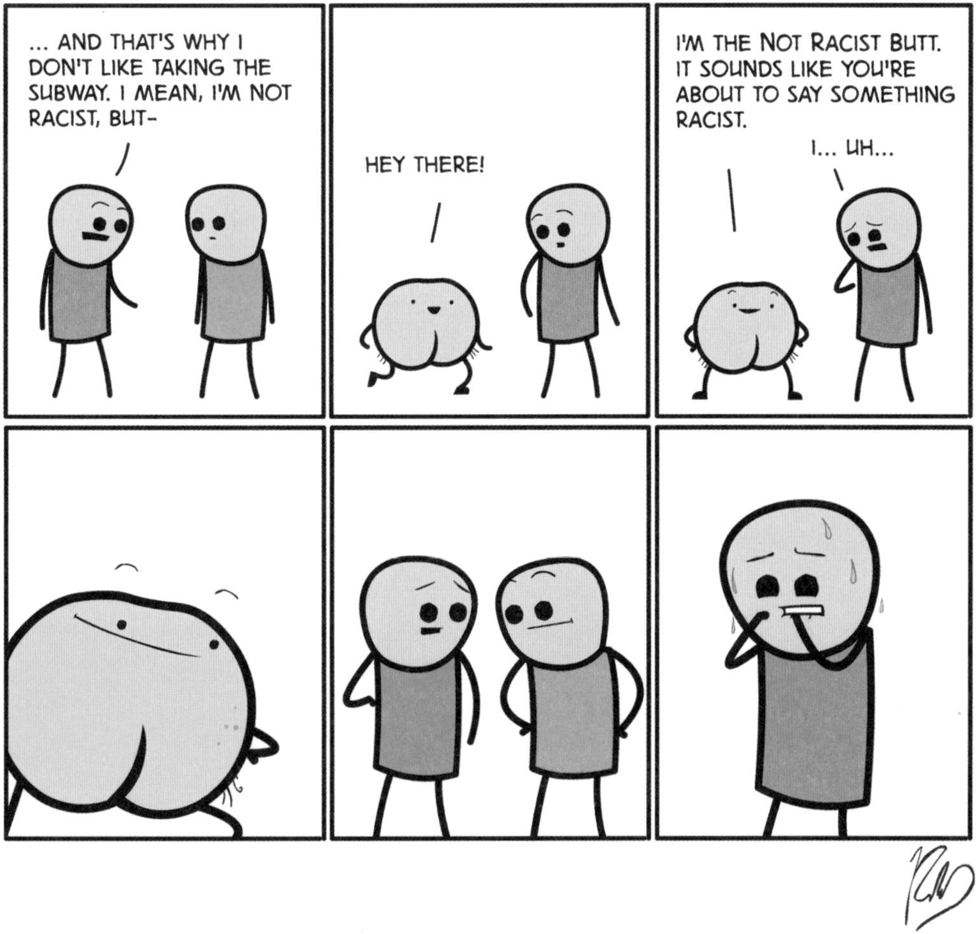
... AND THAT'S WHY I DON'T LIKE TAKING THE SUBWAY. I MEAN, I'M NOT RACIST, BUT-
HEY THERE!
I'M THE NOT RACIST BUTT. IT SOUNDS LIKE YOU'RE ABOUT TO SAY SOMETHING RACIST.
I... UH...

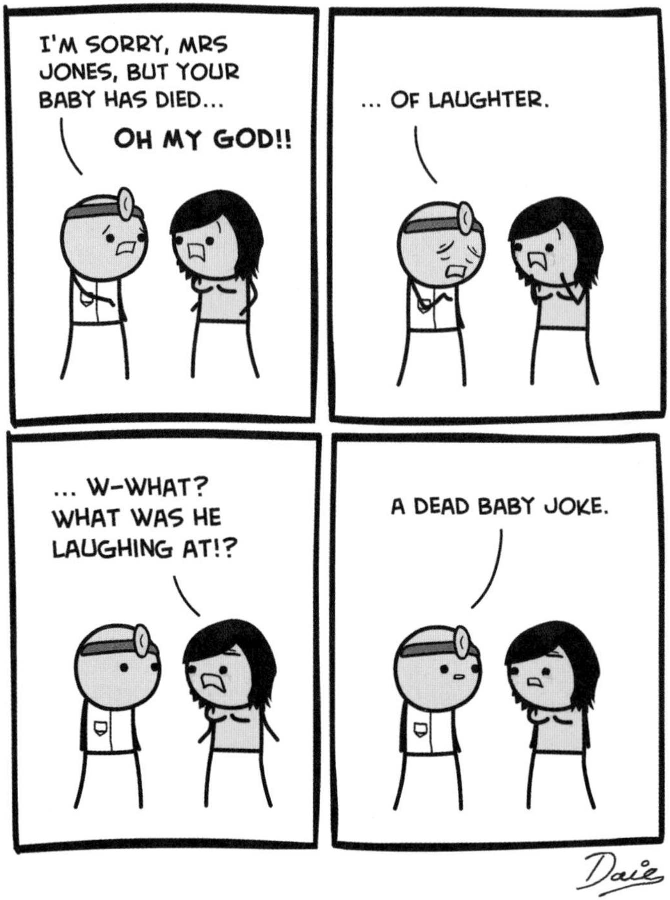
I'M SORRY, MRS JONES, BUT YOUR BABY HAS DIED...
OH MY GOD!!
... OF LAUGHTER.
... W-WHAT? WHAT WAS HE LAUGHING AT!?
A DEAD BABY JOKE.
Dave

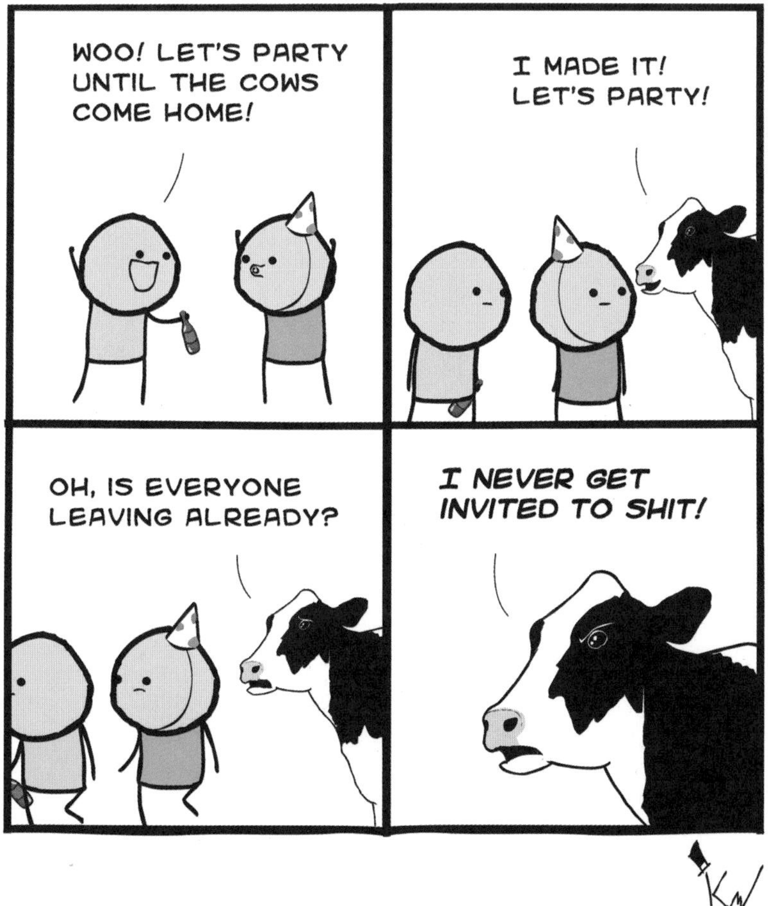
WOO! LET'S PARTY UNTIL THE COWS COME HOME!
I MADE IT! LET'S PARTY!
OH, IS EVERYONE LEAVING ALREADY?
I NEVER GET INVITED TO SHIT!

YOU SON OF A BITCH! YOU'VE BEEN SLEEPING WITH MY WIFE!
YEP.
HOW DO YOU SLEEP AT NIGHT?!
WITH YOUR WIFE.

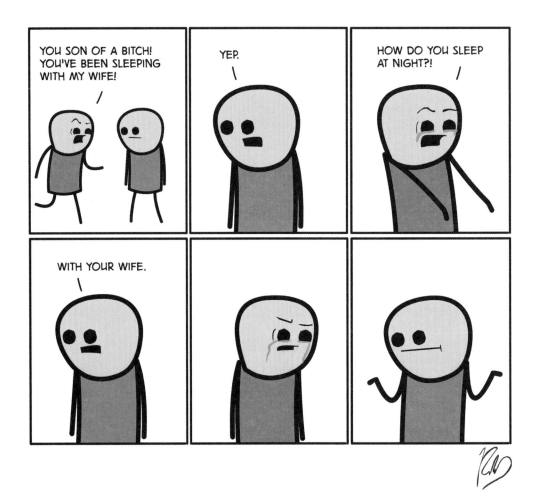

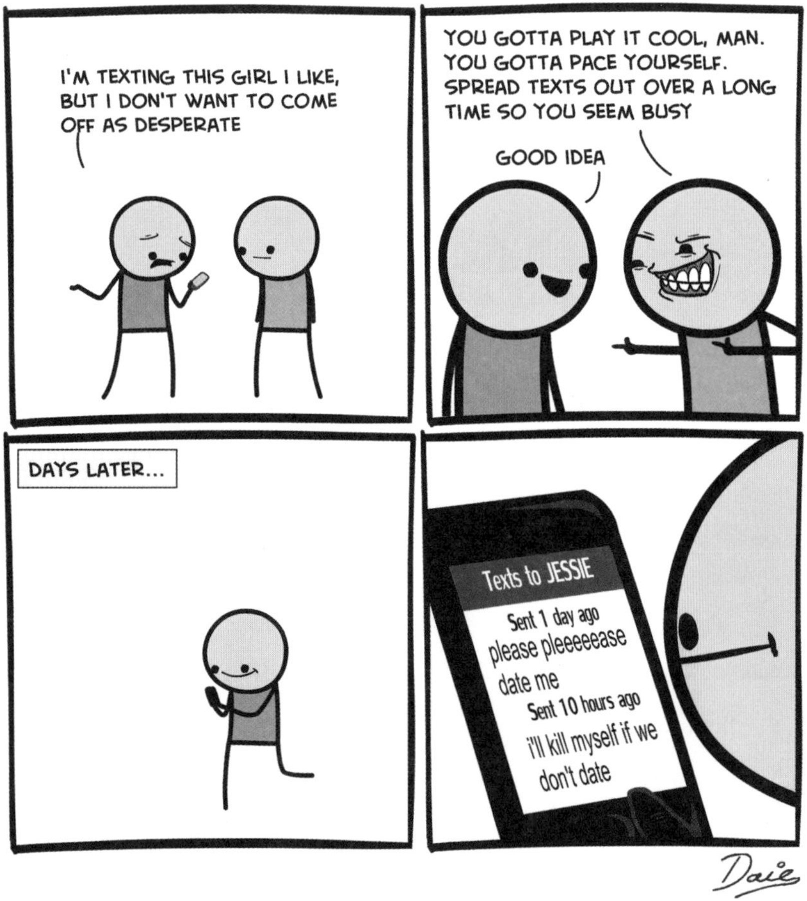
I'M TEXTING THIS GIRL I LIKE, BUT I DON'T WANT TO COME OFF AS DESPERATE
YOU GOTTA PLAY IT COOL, MAN. YOU GOTTA PACE YOURSELF. SPREAD TEXTS OUT OVER A LONG TIME SO YOU SEEM BUSY
GOOD IDEA
DAYS LATER...
Texts to JESSIE
Sent 1 day ago
please pleeeeease date me
Sent 10 hours ago
i'll kill myself if we don't date
Dave

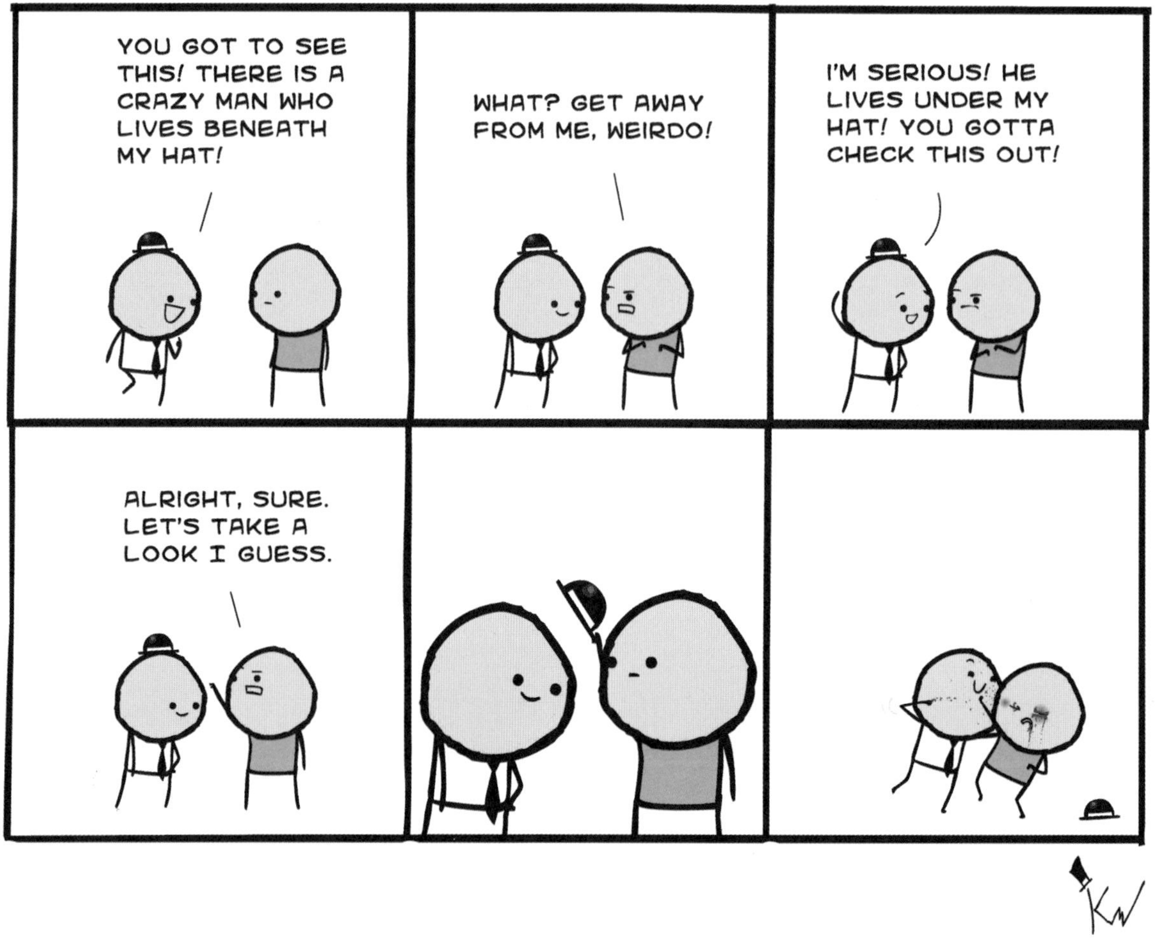
YOU GOT TO SEE THIS! THERE IS A CRAZY MAN WHO LIVES BENEATH MY HAT!
WHAT? GET AWAY FROM ME, WEIRDO!
I'M SERIOUS! HE LIVES UNDER MY HAT! YOU GOTTA CHECK THIS OUT!
ALRIGHT, SURE. LET'S TAKE A LOOK I GUESS.

HEY YOU! IT'S NOT SAFE TO SMOKE BY A GAS PUMP.

TECHNICALLY IT'S NOT SAFE TO SMOKE ANYWHERE.

HONEY, THE DOCTOR SAYS IF I DON'T HAVE BUTTSEX AT LEAST FIVE TIMES A WEEK, I'LL DIE.

WOW, ARE YOU SERIOUS? THIS IS THE SORRIEST ATTEMPT I'VE HEARD FROM YOU YET.

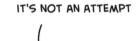

IT'S NOT AN ATTEMPT

HE WANTS ME TO GO BACK IN TOMORROW.

Daie

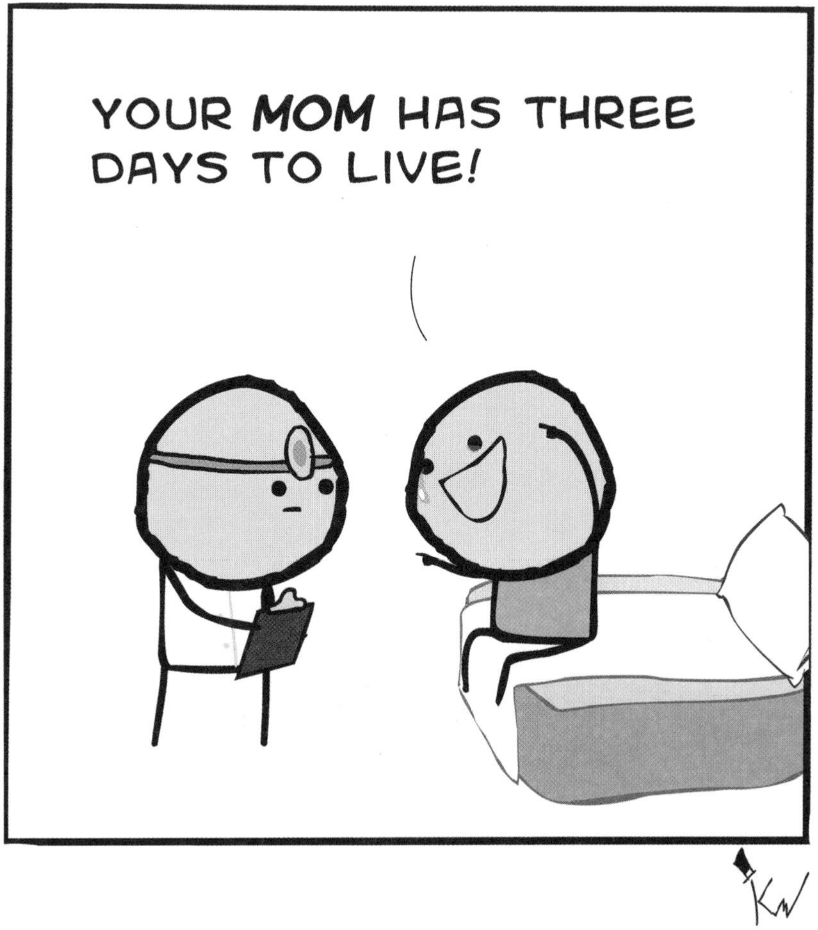
YOUR **MOM** HAS THREE DAYS TO LIVE!
KW

HEY HONEY. SO I WAS DOING SOME MATH.
IF YOU'RE EIGHT MONTHS PREGNANT...
AND WE ONLY MET SIX MONTHS AGO...
AND I'M ON A TRAIN TRAVELING FIFTY MILES PER HOUR...
AND YOU SOLD ME FOUR APPLES...
THEN WHERE THE HELL ARE MY APPLES?

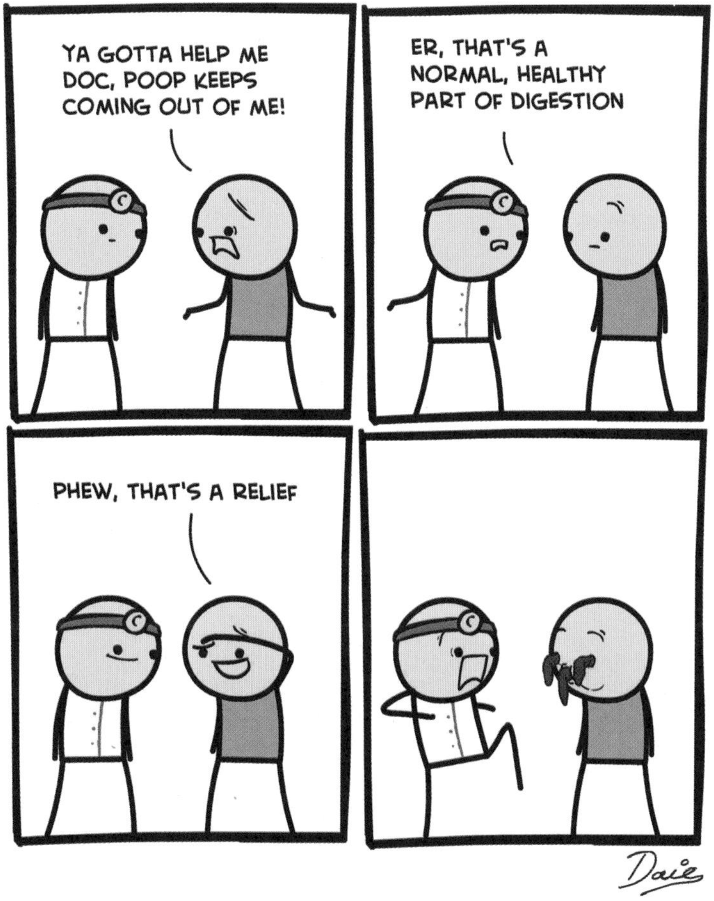
YA GOTTA HELP ME DOC, POOP KEEPS COMING OUT OF ME!
ER, THAT'S A NORMAL, HEALTHY PART OF DIGESTION
PHEW, THAT'S A RELIEF
Dave

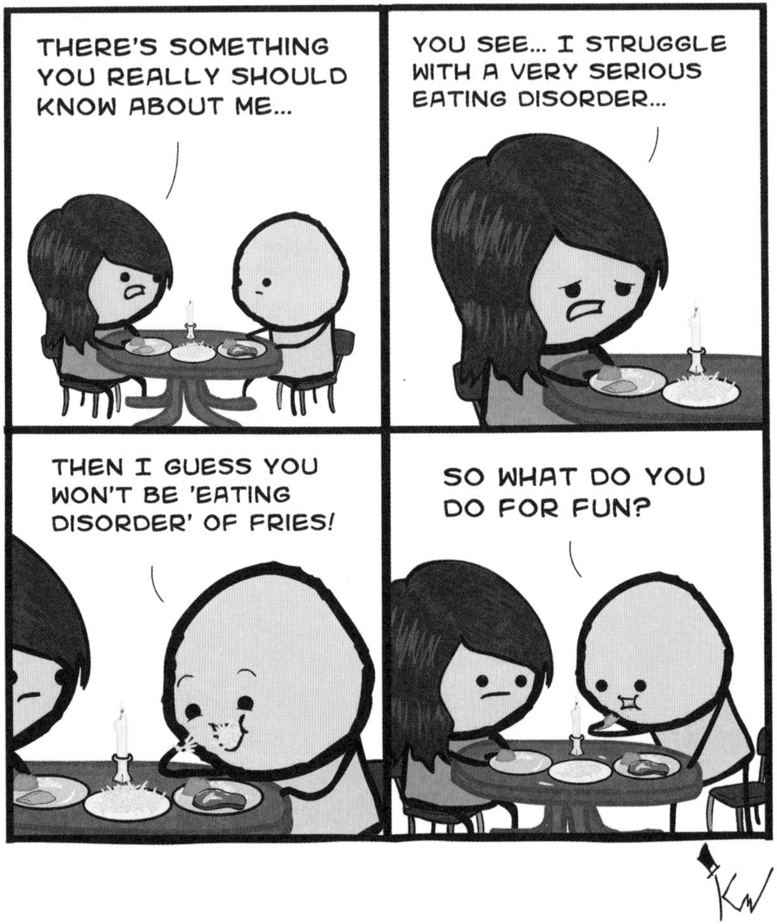
THERE'S SOMETHING YOU REALLY SHOULD KNOW ABOUT ME...
YOU SEE... I STRUGGLE WITH A VERY SERIOUS EATING DISORDER...
THEN I GUESS YOU WON'T BE 'EATING DISORDER' OF FRIES!
SO WHAT DO YOU DO FOR FUN?

DAMN IT, DOG!
THAT'S IT... I'M GETTING THE NEWSPAPER!
THE DAILY PAPER
Kill Shelters on Rise

I JUST CAME INTO A TON OF MONEY, CHECK IT OUT!
WHOA, WHERE'D YOU GET IT?
I ALREADY HAD IT, I JUST NOW CAME INTO IT
WITH
MY
DICK
Dave

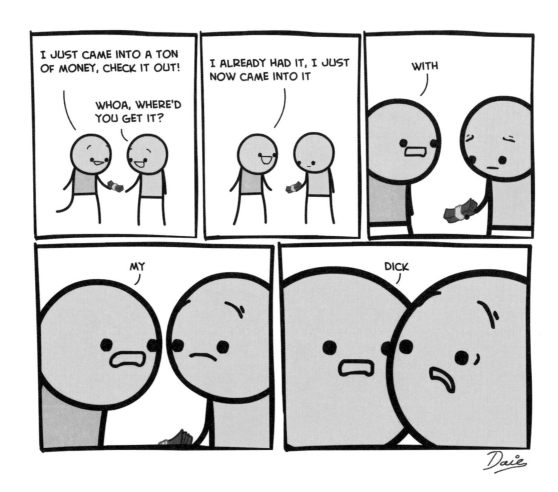

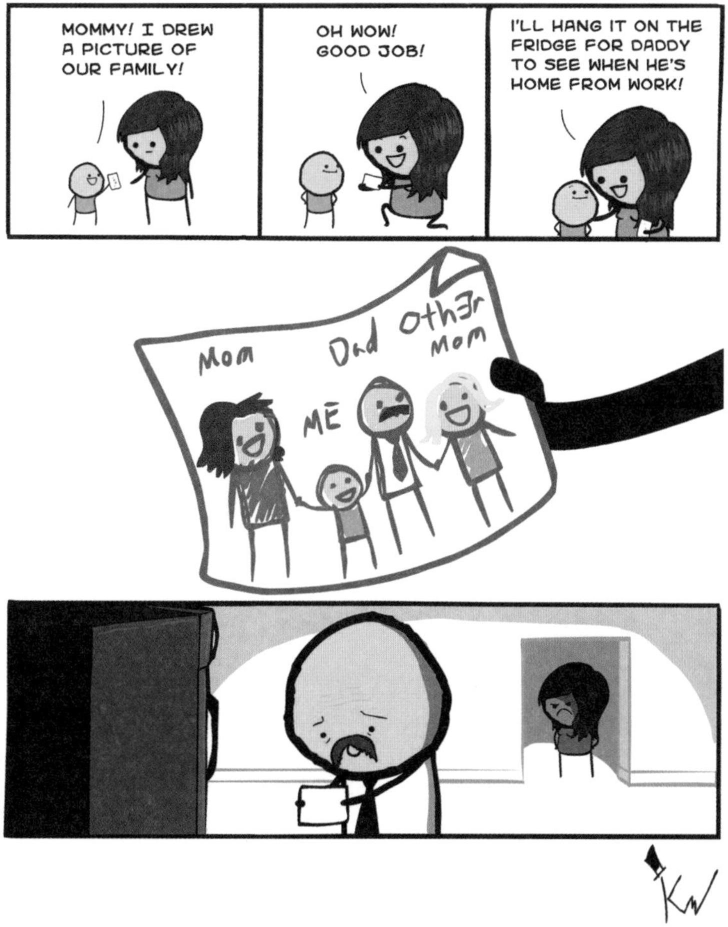
MOMMY! I DREW A PICTURE OF OUR FAMILY!
OH WOW! GOOD JOB!
I'LL HANG IT ON THE FRIDGE FOR DADDY TO SEE WHEN HE'S HOME FROM WORK!
Mom
Dad
Oth3r Mom
ME

HEY MAN... YOU'RE GOOD WITH THE LADIES. HOW DO I TELL IF THIS GIRL I'M TEXTING IS INTO ME?
DUDE... JUST SEND HER YOUR DICK AND SEE HOW SHE RESPONDS.

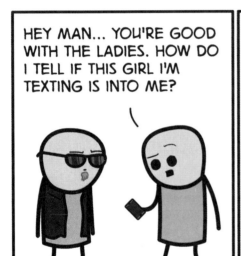

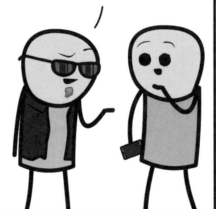

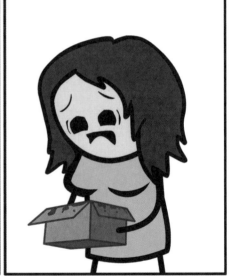

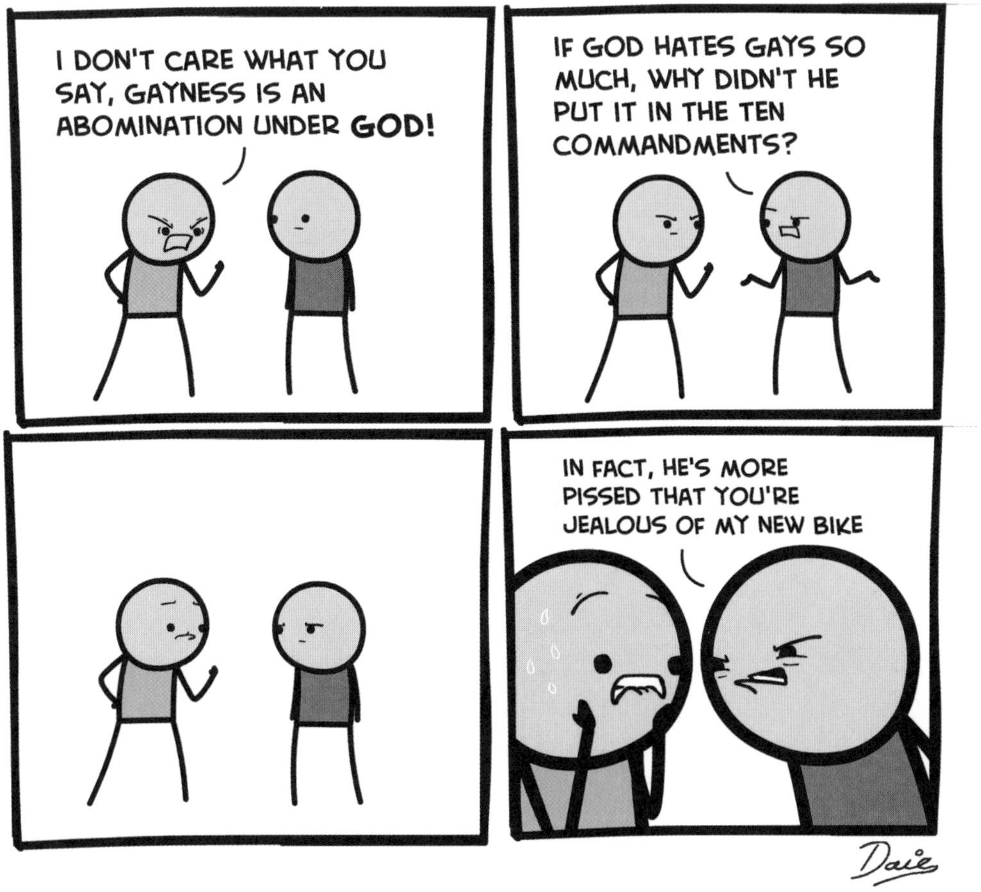
I DON'T CARE WHAT YOU SAY, GAYNESS IS AN ABOMINATION UNDER GOD!
IF GOD HATES GAYS SO MUCH, WHY DIDN'T HE PUT IT IN THE TEN COMMANDMENTS?
IN FACT, HE'S MORE PISSED THAT YOU'RE JEALOUS OF MY NEW BIKE
Dave

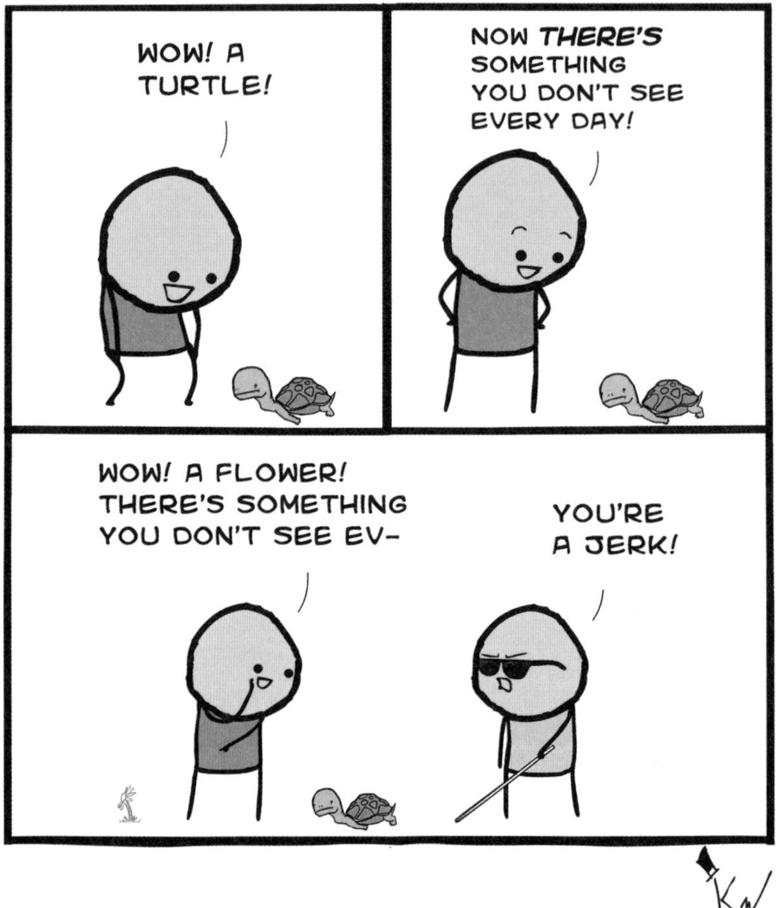
WOW! A TURTLE!
NOW *THERE'S* SOMETHING YOU DON'T SEE EVERY DAY!
WOW! A FLOWER! THERE'S SOMETHING YOU DON'T SEE EV–
YOU'RE A JERK!

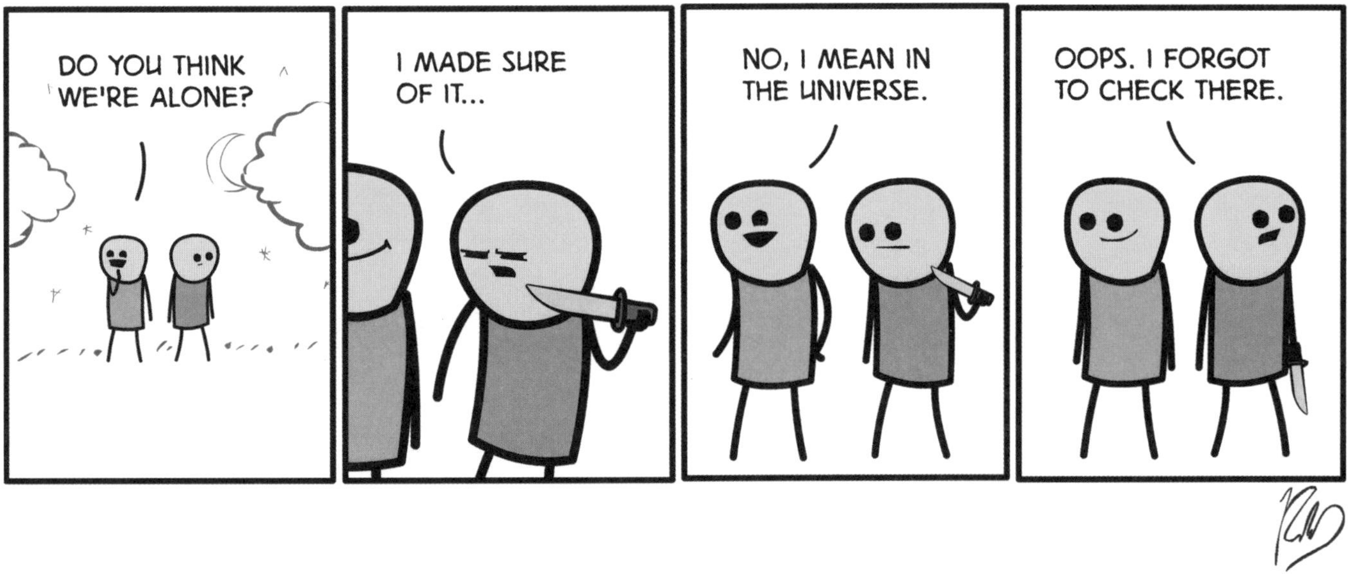
DO YOU THINK WE'RE ALONE?
I MADE SURE OF IT...
NO, I MEAN IN THE UNIVERSE.
OOPS. I FORGOT TO CHECK THERE.

CONGRATUMALATIONS, YOU HAVE WON A **GOLDEN SHOWER!**
HOORAY! WAIT, WHAT DO YOU MEAN BY GOLDEN SHOWER?
AWWWW
Dave

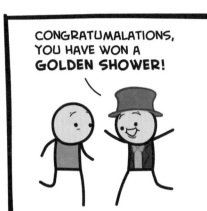

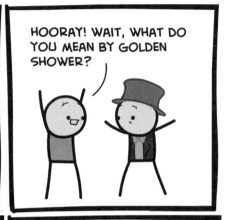

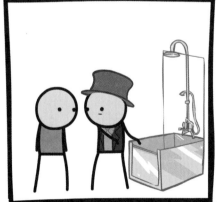

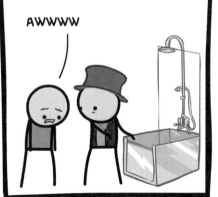

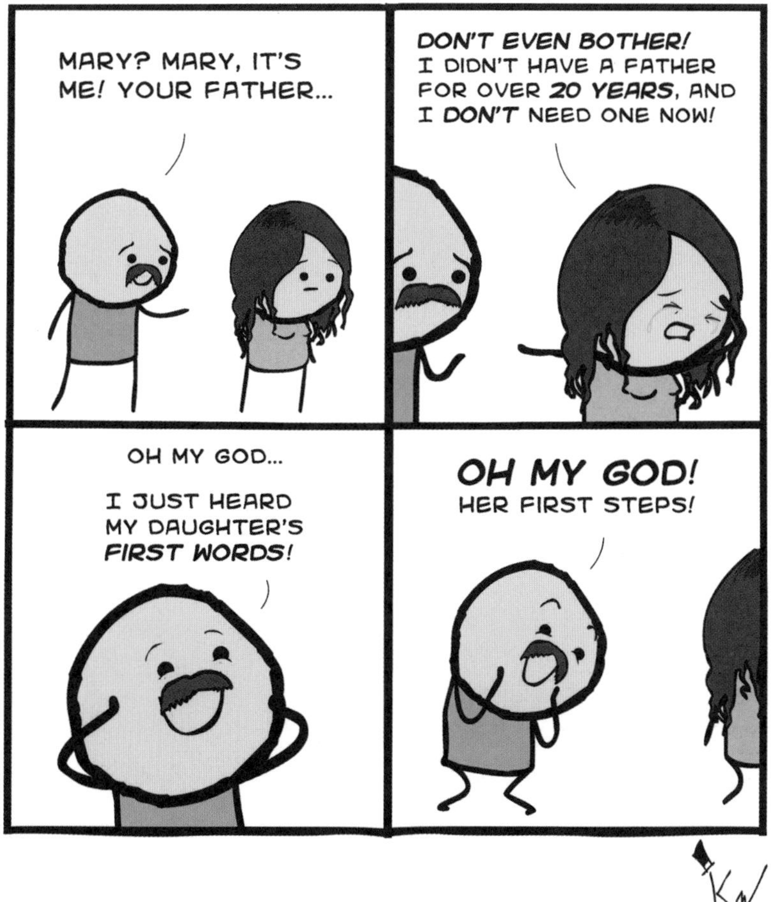
MARY? MARY, IT'S ME! YOUR FATHER...
DON'T EVEN BOTHER! I DIDN'T HAVE A FATHER FOR OVER 20 YEARS, AND I DON'T NEED ONE NOW!
OH MY GOD...
I JUST HEARD MY DAUGHTER'S FIRST WORDS!
OH MY GOD! HER FIRST STEPS!

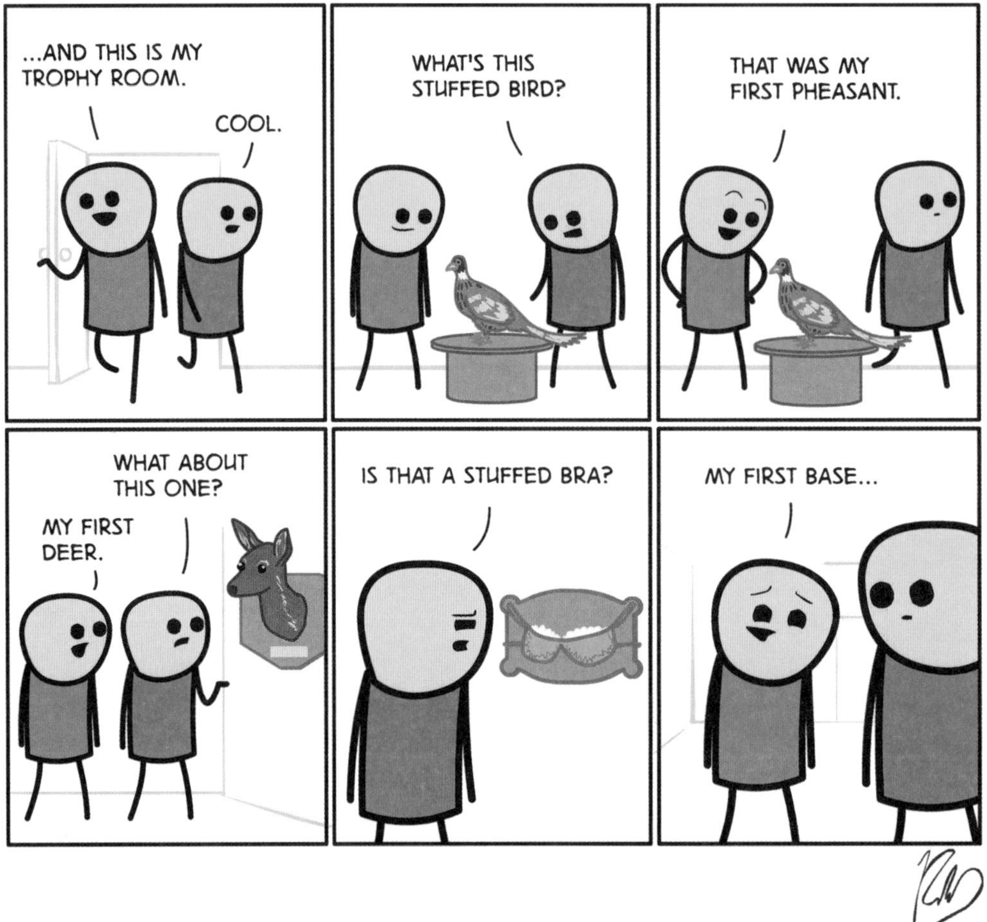
...AND THIS IS MY TROPHY ROOM.
COOL.
WHAT'S THIS STUFFED BIRD?
THAT WAS MY FIRST PHEASANT.
WHAT ABOUT THIS ONE?
MY FIRST DEER.
IS THAT A STUFFED BRA?
MY FIRST BASE...

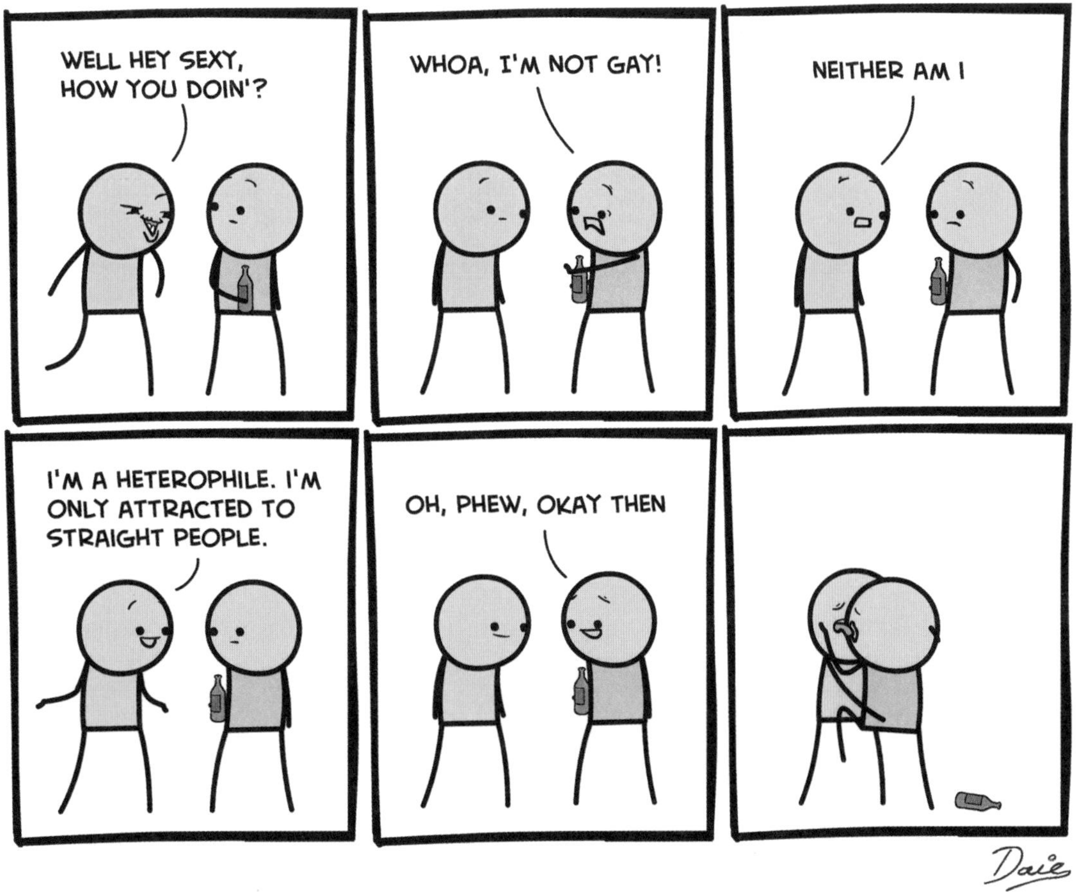
WELL HEY SEXY, HOW YOU DOIN'?
WHOA, I'M NOT GAY!
NEITHER AM I
I'M A HETEROPHILE. I'M ONLY ATTRACTED TO STRAIGHT PEOPLE.
OH, PHEW, OKAY THEN
Dave

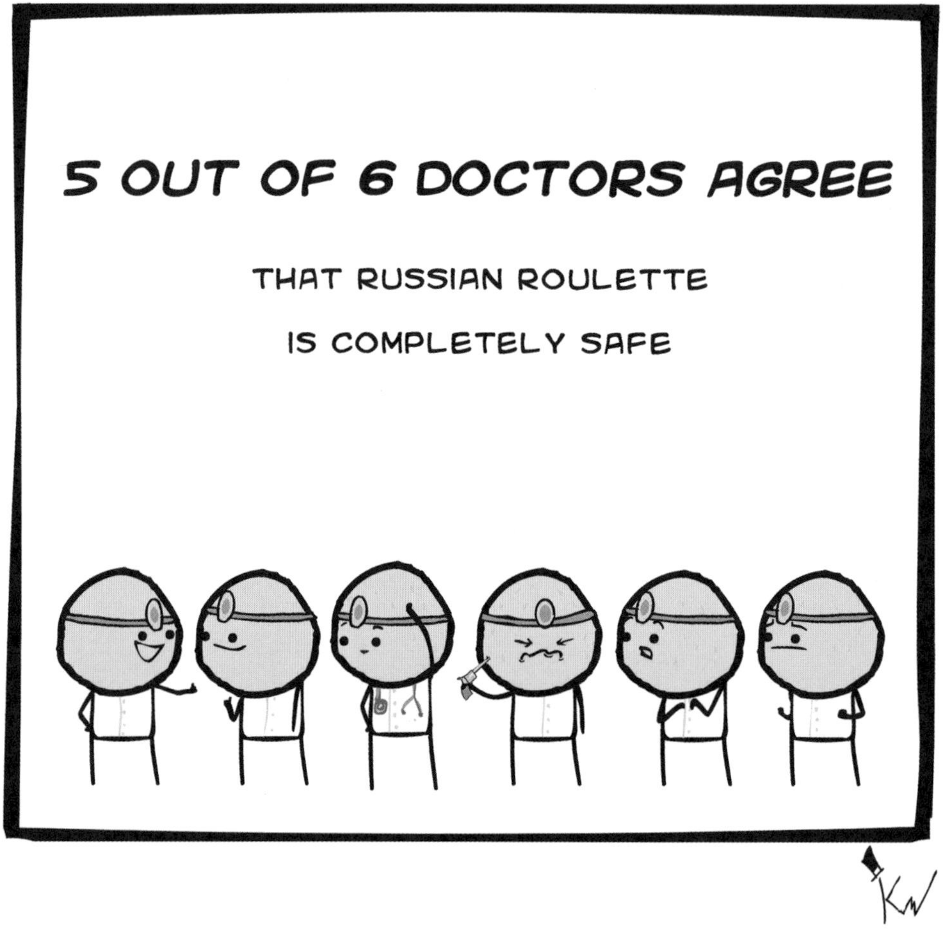
5 OUT OF 6 DOCTORS AGREE
THAT RUSSIAN ROULETTE
IS COMPLETELY SAFE
KW

WHERE DO BABIES COME FROM?
YOUR MOM!
AS FAR AS I KNOW.

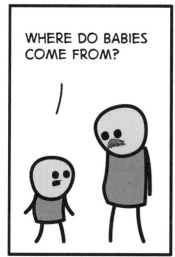

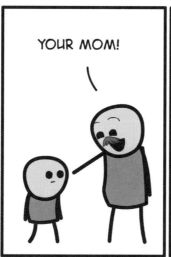

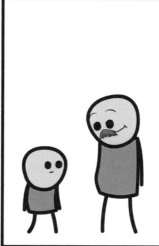

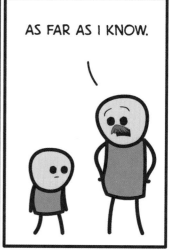

I DON'T LIKE STEVE, HE'S CREEPY.
I AGREE.
HELLO FRIENDS, I MADE US CUPCAKES!
WHAT DID I SAY...?
Dave

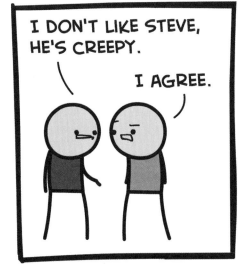

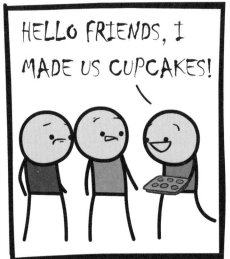

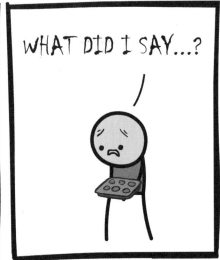

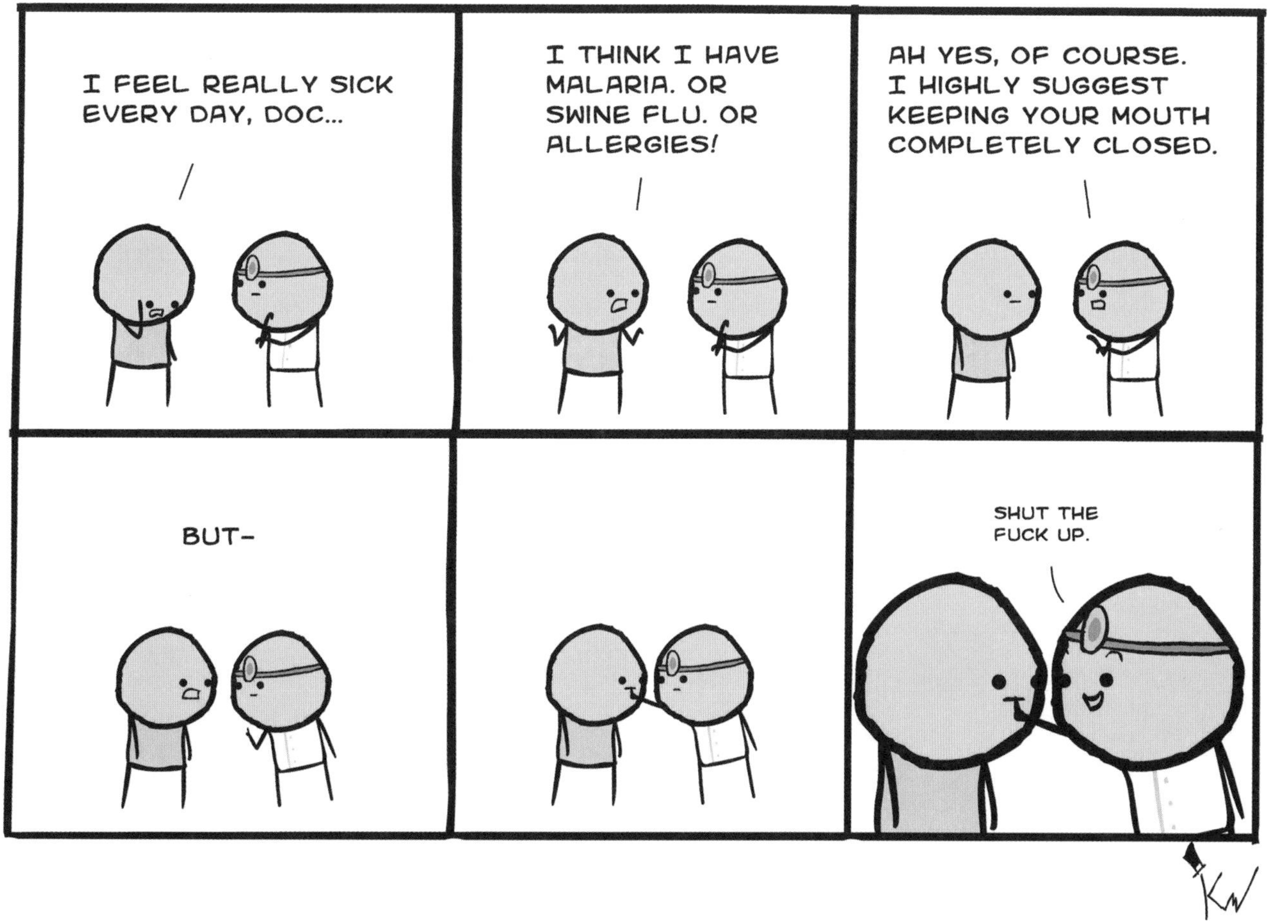
I FEEL REALLY SICK EVERY DAY, DOC...
I THINK I HAVE MALARIA. OR SWINE FLU. OR ALLERGIES!
AH YES, OF COURSE. I HIGHLY SUGGEST KEEPING YOUR MOUTH COMPLETELY CLOSED.
BUT-
SHUT THE FUCK UP.

THE ADVENTURES OF
HERBERT
THE
ZOMBIE HOBO!

BRAAAAINS...

SORRY MAN, I
DON'T HAVE ANY.

WELL, WE'VE GOT YOUR X-RAYS BACK
AND WE CAN SEE ABSOLUTELY NOTHING. YOU'RE GOOD TO GO.
AWESOME, HAVE A GOOD DAY.
Dave

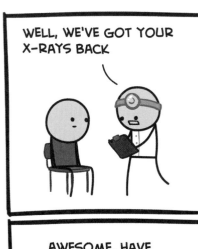

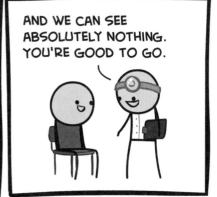

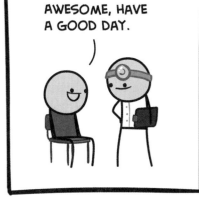

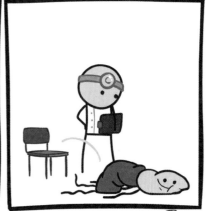

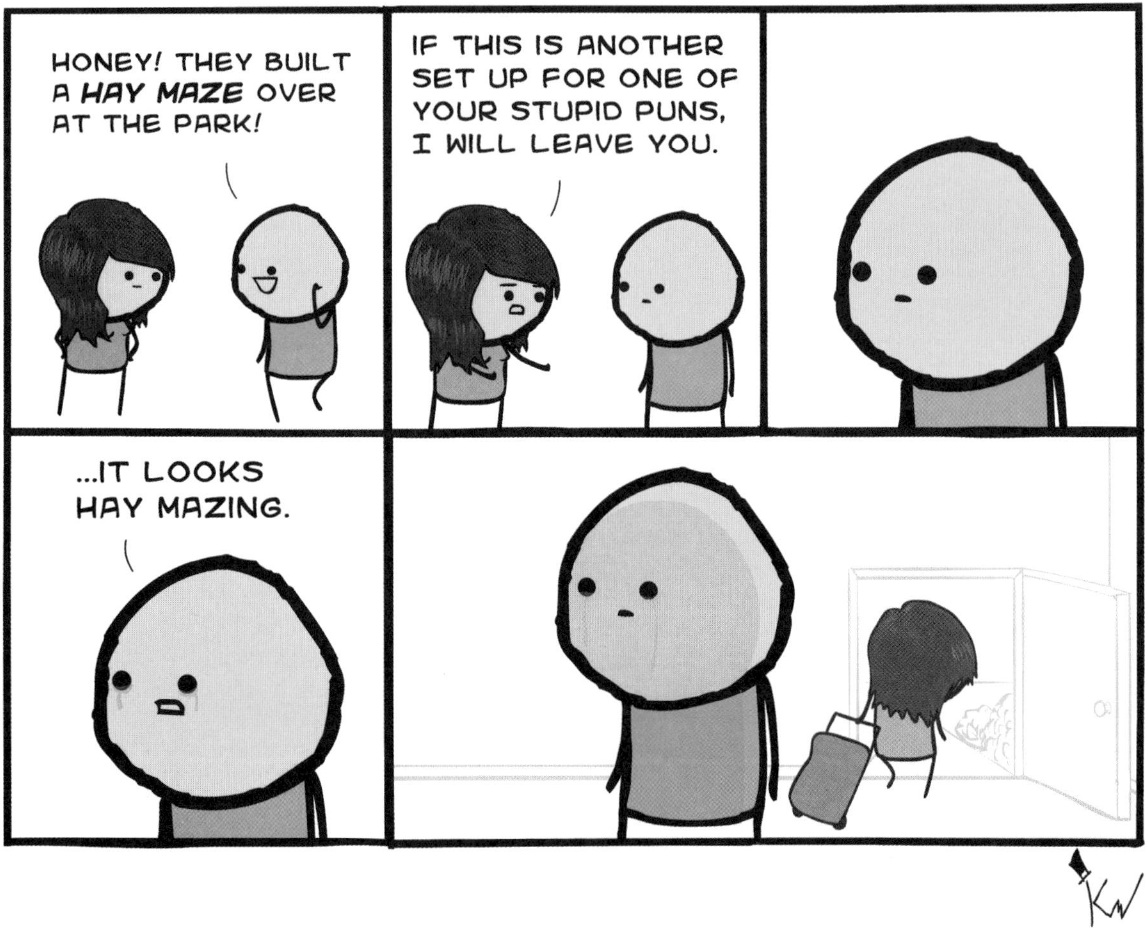
HONEY! THEY BUILT A **HAY MAZE** OVER AT THE PARK!
IF THIS IS ANOTHER SET UP FOR ONE OF YOUR STUPID PUNS, I WILL LEAVE YOU.
...IT LOOKS HAY MAZING.
KW

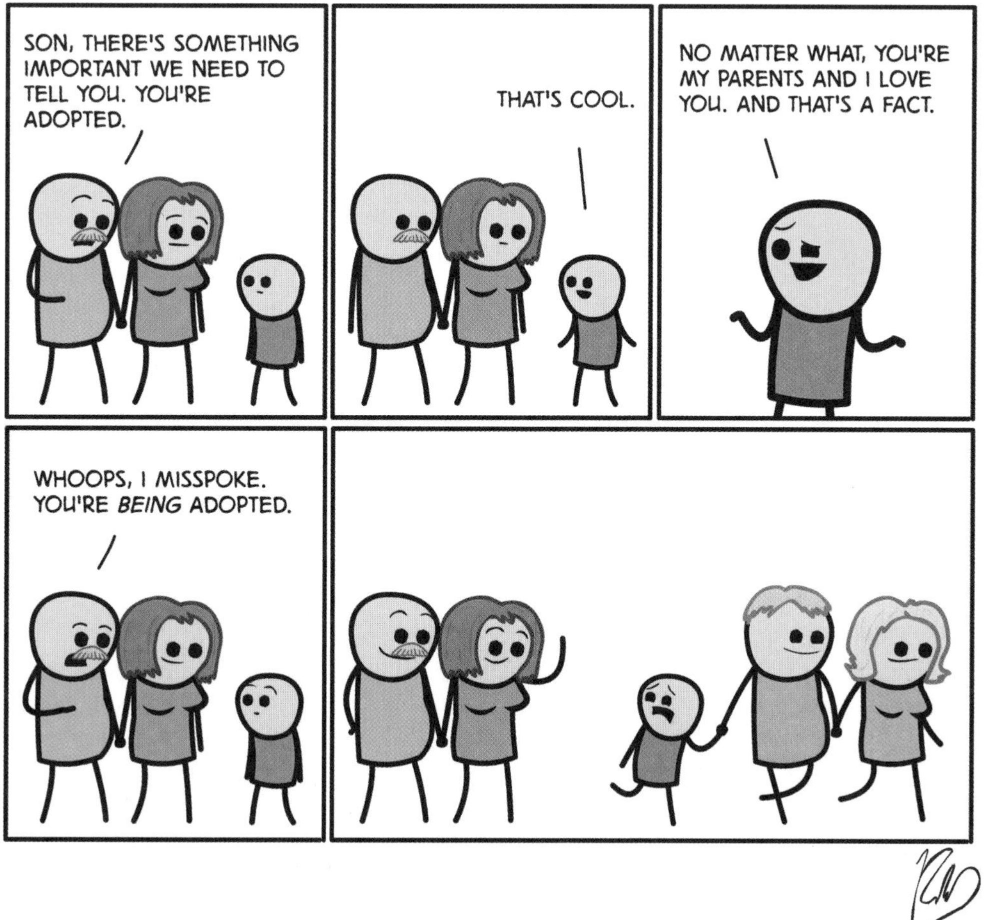
SON, THERE'S SOMETHING IMPORTANT WE NEED TO TELL YOU. YOU'RE ADOPTED.
THAT'S COOL.
NO MATTER WHAT, YOU'RE MY PARENTS AND I LOVE YOU. AND THAT'S A FACT.
WHOOPS, I MISSPOKE. YOU'RE *BEING* ADOPTED.

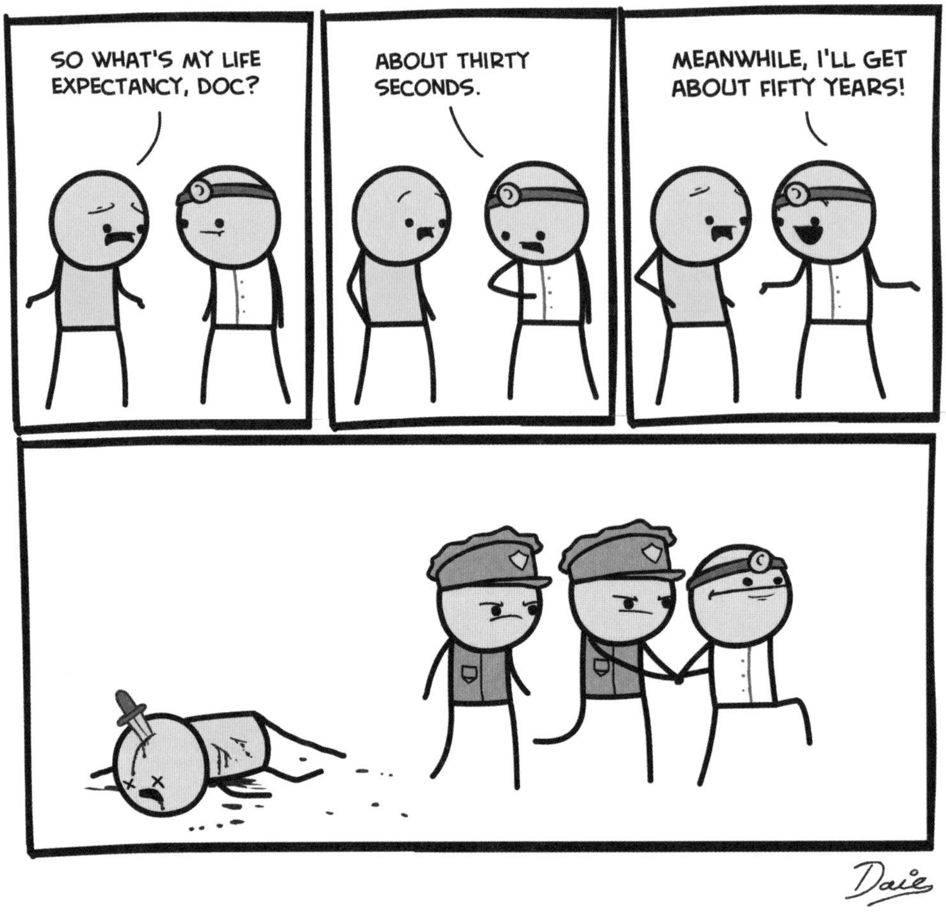
SO WHAT'S MY LIFE EXPECTANCY, DOC?
ABOUT THIRTY SECONDS.
MEANWHILE, I'LL GET ABOUT FIFTY YEARS!
Dave

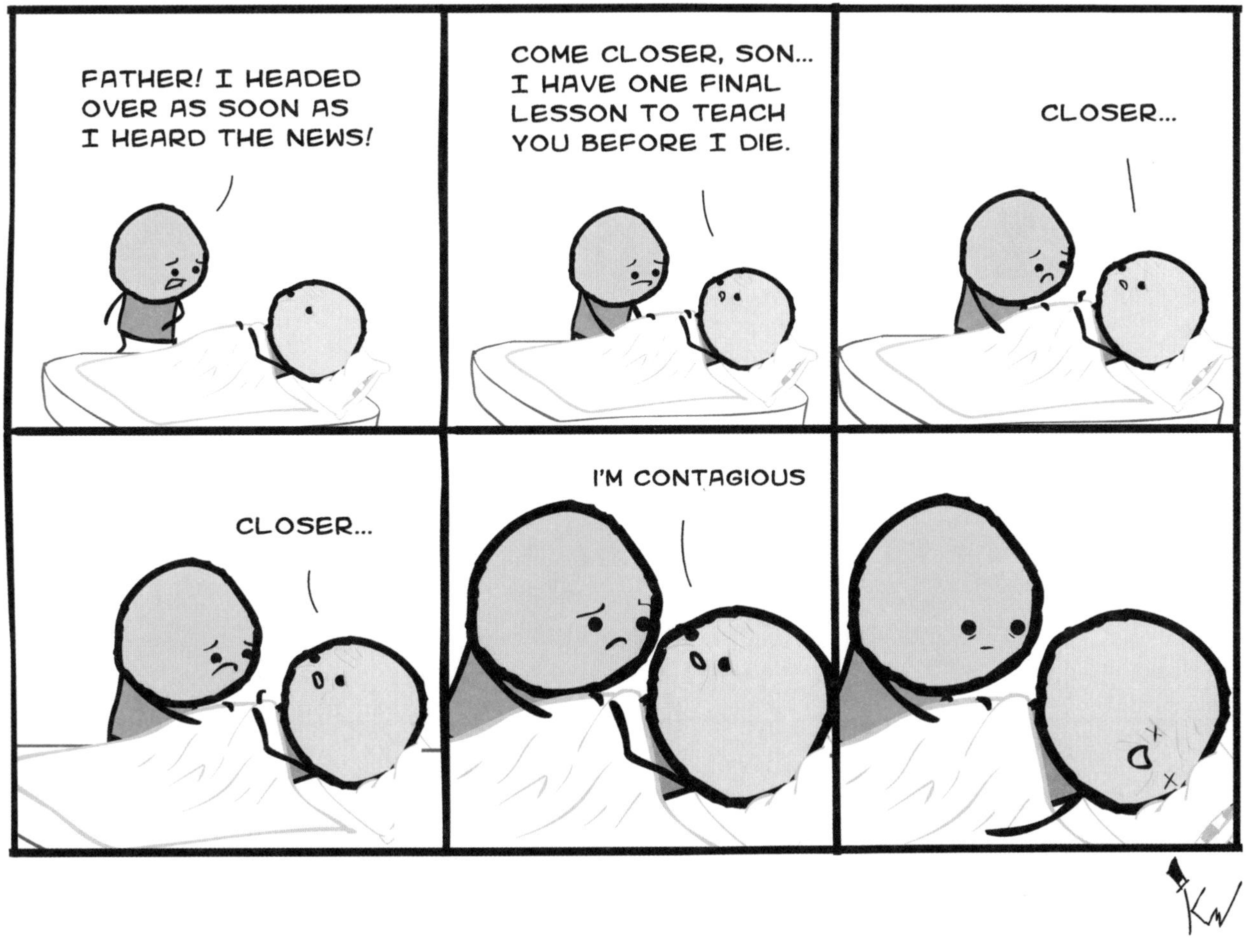
FATHER! I HEADED OVER AS SOON AS I HEARD THE NEWS!
COME CLOSER, SON... I HAVE ONE FINAL LESSON TO TEACH YOU BEFORE I DIE.
CLOSER...
CLOSER...
I'M CONTAGIOUS
KW

ALOE YOU VERA MUCH!

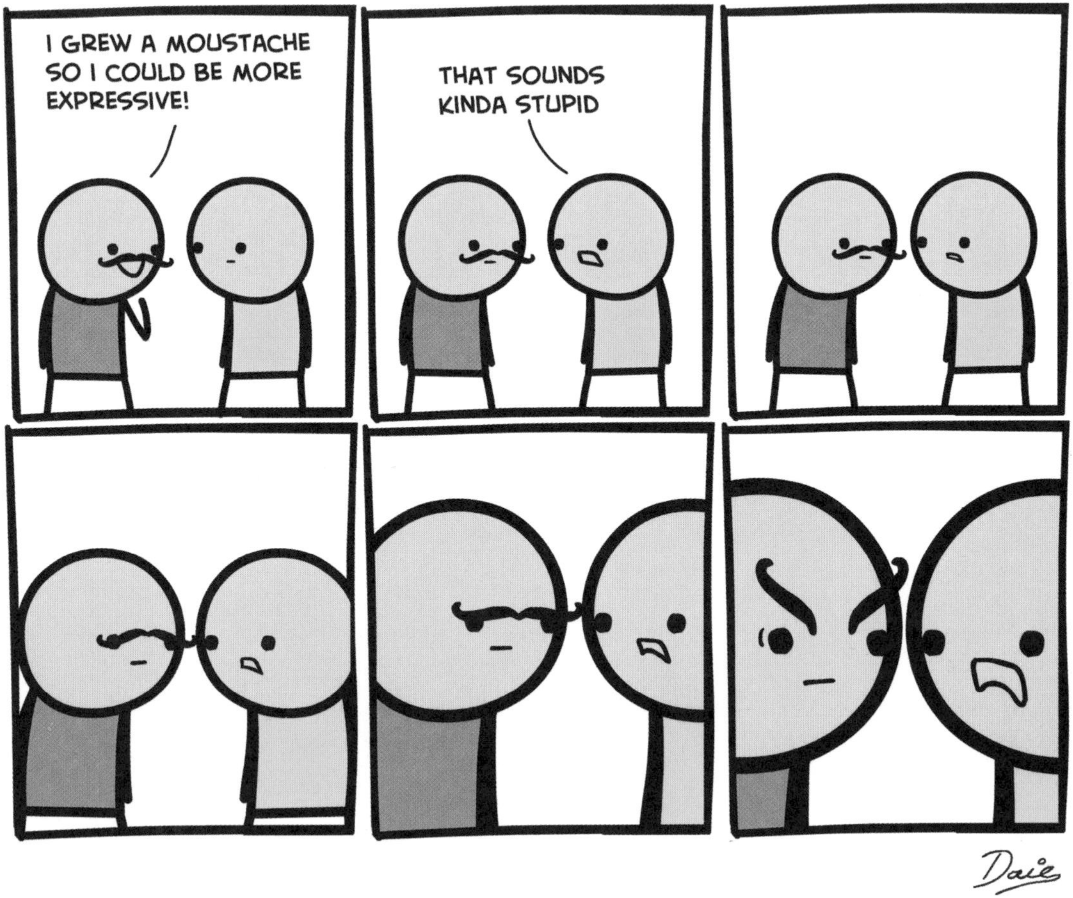
I GREW A MOUSTACHE SO I COULD BE MORE EXPRESSIVE!
THAT SOUNDS KINDA STUPID
Dave

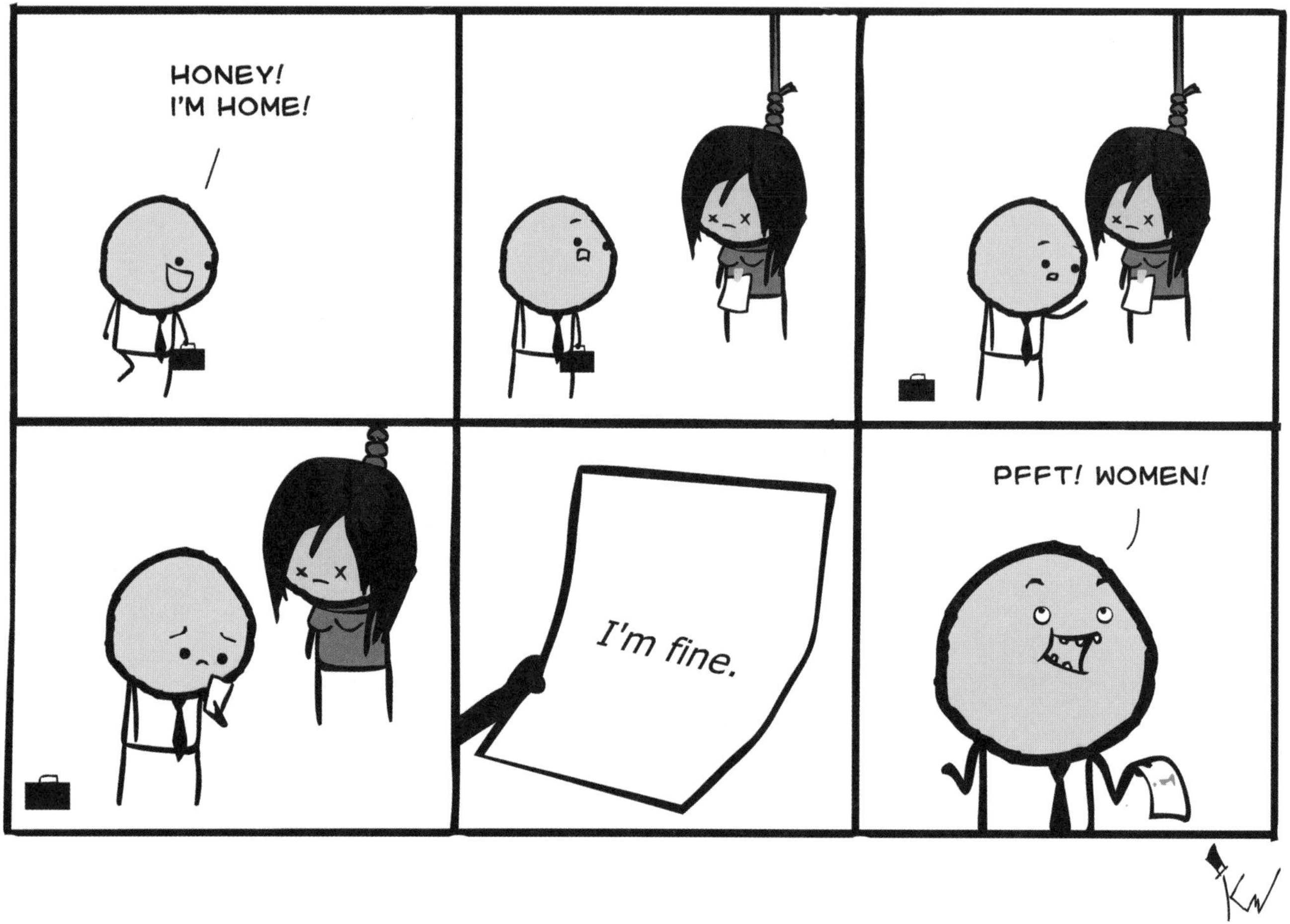
HONEY!
I'M HOME!
I'm fine.
PFFT! WOMEN!

SON, TODAY'S THE DAY YOU BECOME A MAN.
AND I BECOME A BOY.

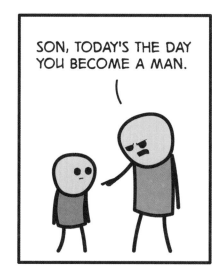

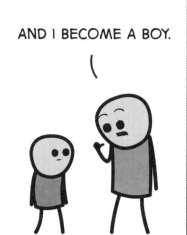

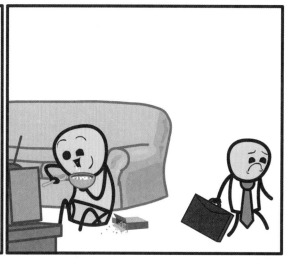

UH... HI. MY NAME IS JOE, AND I'M AN ALCOHOLIC.
NO YOU'RE NOT.
Liars Anonymous
KW

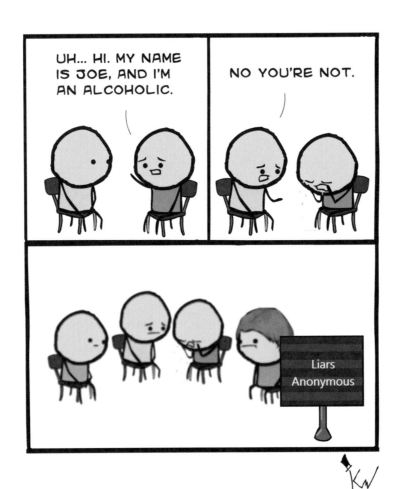

ME? I'M KIND OF AN ASS MAN MYSELF.
REALLY? I'M MORE OF A BOOBS MAN.
I'M A BAT MAN.
THAT'S NOT REALLY WHAT WE WERE TALKING AB-
I FUCK BATS.

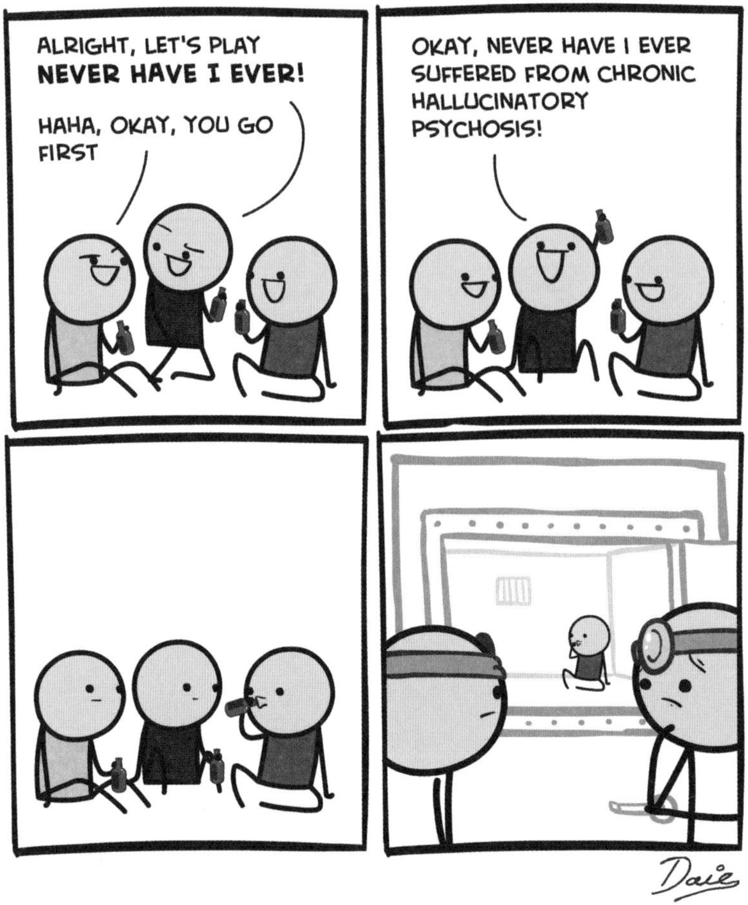
ALRIGHT, LET'S PLAY
NEVER HAVE I EVER!
HAHA, OKAY, YOU GO FIRST
OKAY, NEVER HAVE I EVER SUFFERED FROM CHRONIC HALLUCINATORY PSYCHOSIS!
Dave

DAD! DAD! THE GROUND IS LAVA!
DON'T TOUCH THE FLOOR OR ELSE YOU'LL MELT!
SON, I THINK YOUR MUSHROOMS KICKED IN BEFORE MINE DID.
KW

UGHH... BLUH...

ALRIGHT, BUDDY... IT'S INTO THE DRUNK TANK WITH YOU.

YES, YOU ARE TECHNICALLY CONSIDERED MORBIDLY OBESE...
... BUT WHAT REALLY MATTERS IS IN *HERE.*
WHAT I'M SAYING IS, YOU HAVE HEART DISEASE.
Dave

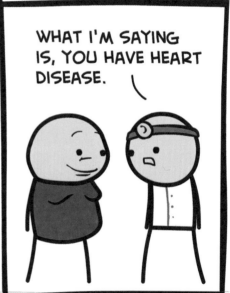

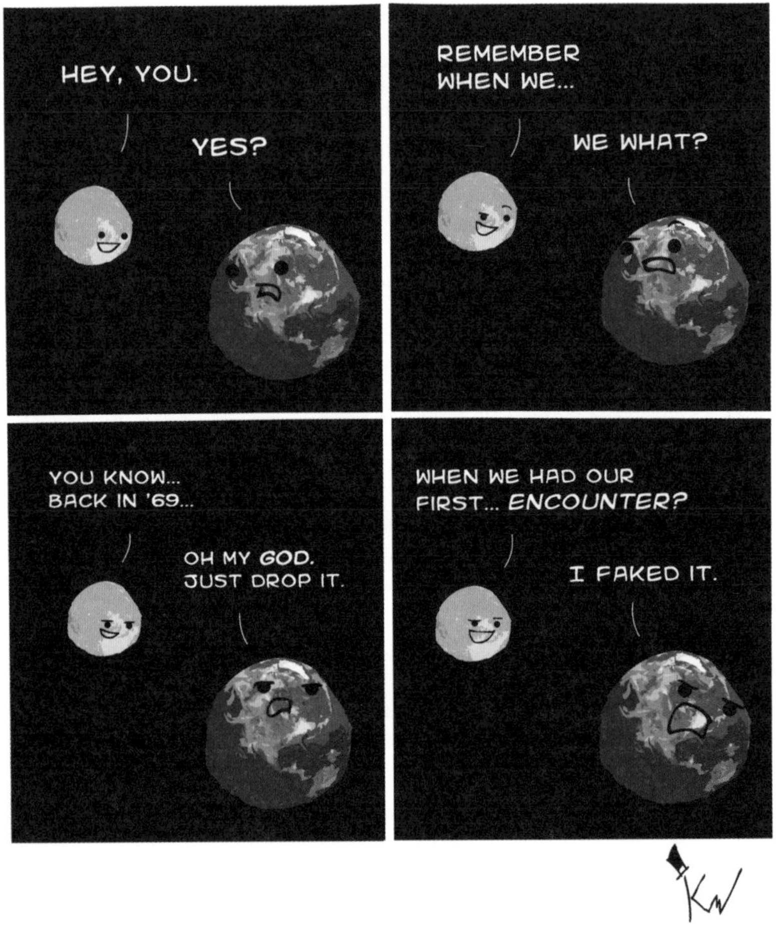
HEY, YOU.
YES?
REMEMBER WHEN WE...
WE WHAT?
YOU KNOW... BACK IN '69...
OH MY GOD. JUST DROP IT.
WHEN WE HAD OUR FIRST... ENCOUNTER?
I FAKED IT.

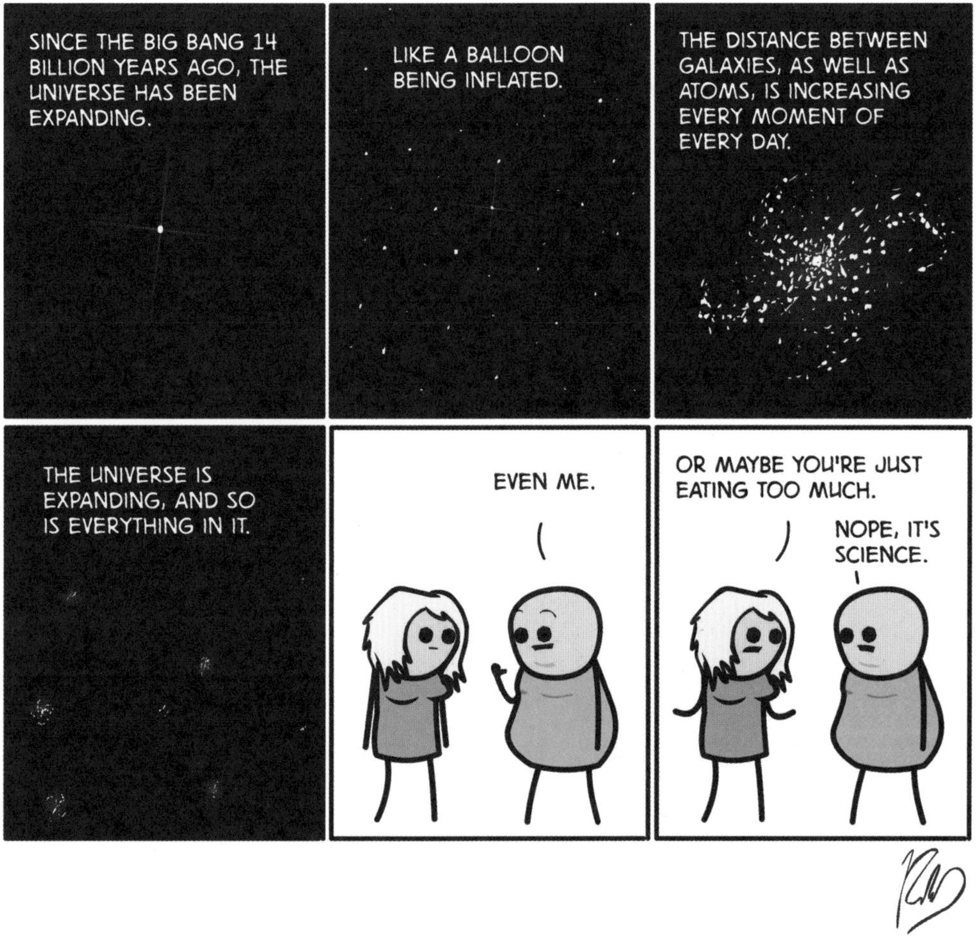
SINCE THE BIG BANG 14 BILLION YEARS AGO, THE UNIVERSE HAS BEEN EXPANDING.
LIKE A BALLOON BEING INFLATED.
THE DISTANCE BETWEEN GALAXIES, AS WELL AS ATOMS, IS INCREASING EVERY MOMENT OF EVERY DAY.
THE UNIVERSE IS EXPANDING, AND SO IS EVERYTHING IN IT.
EVEN ME.
OR MAYBE YOU'RE JUST EATING TOO MUCH.
NOPE, IT'S SCIENCE.

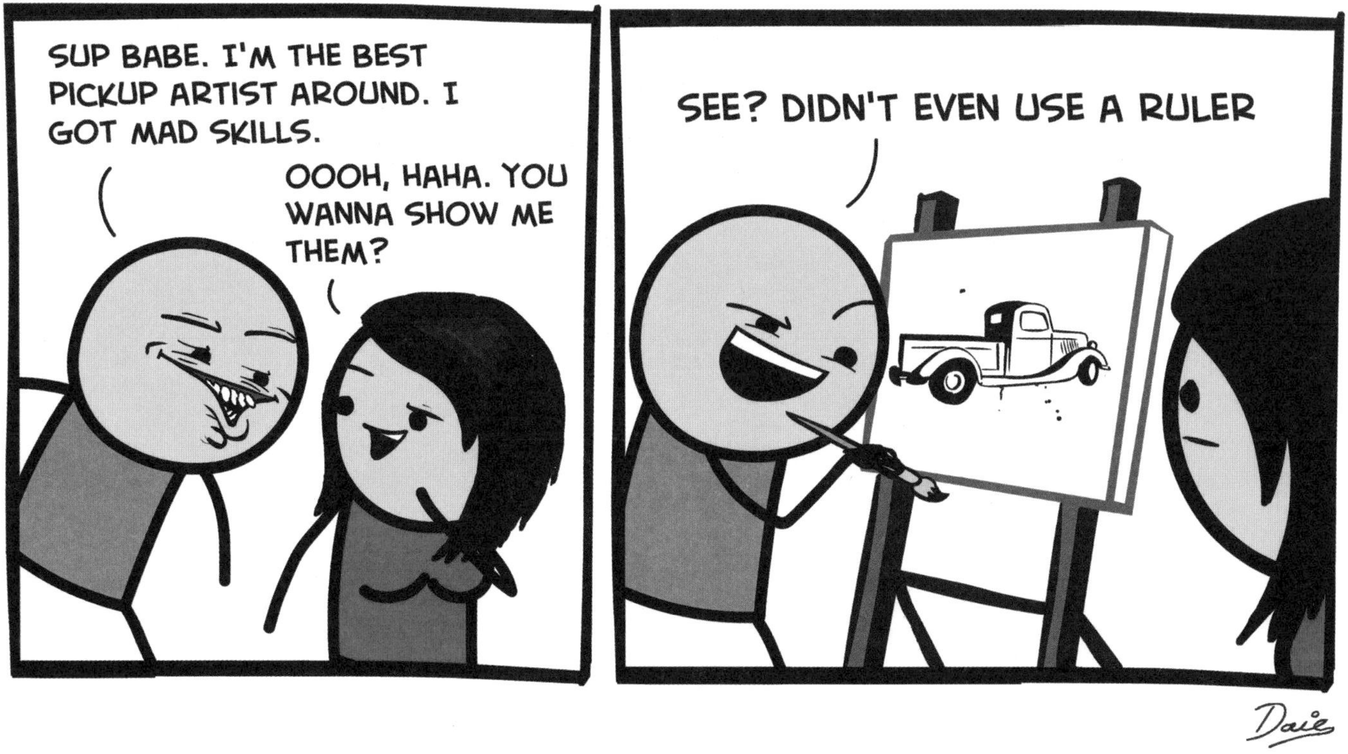
SUP BABE. I'M THE BEST PICKUP ARTIST AROUND. I GOT MAD SKILLS.
OOOH, HAHA. YOU WANNA SHOW ME THEM?
SEE? DIDN'T EVEN USE A RULER
Dave

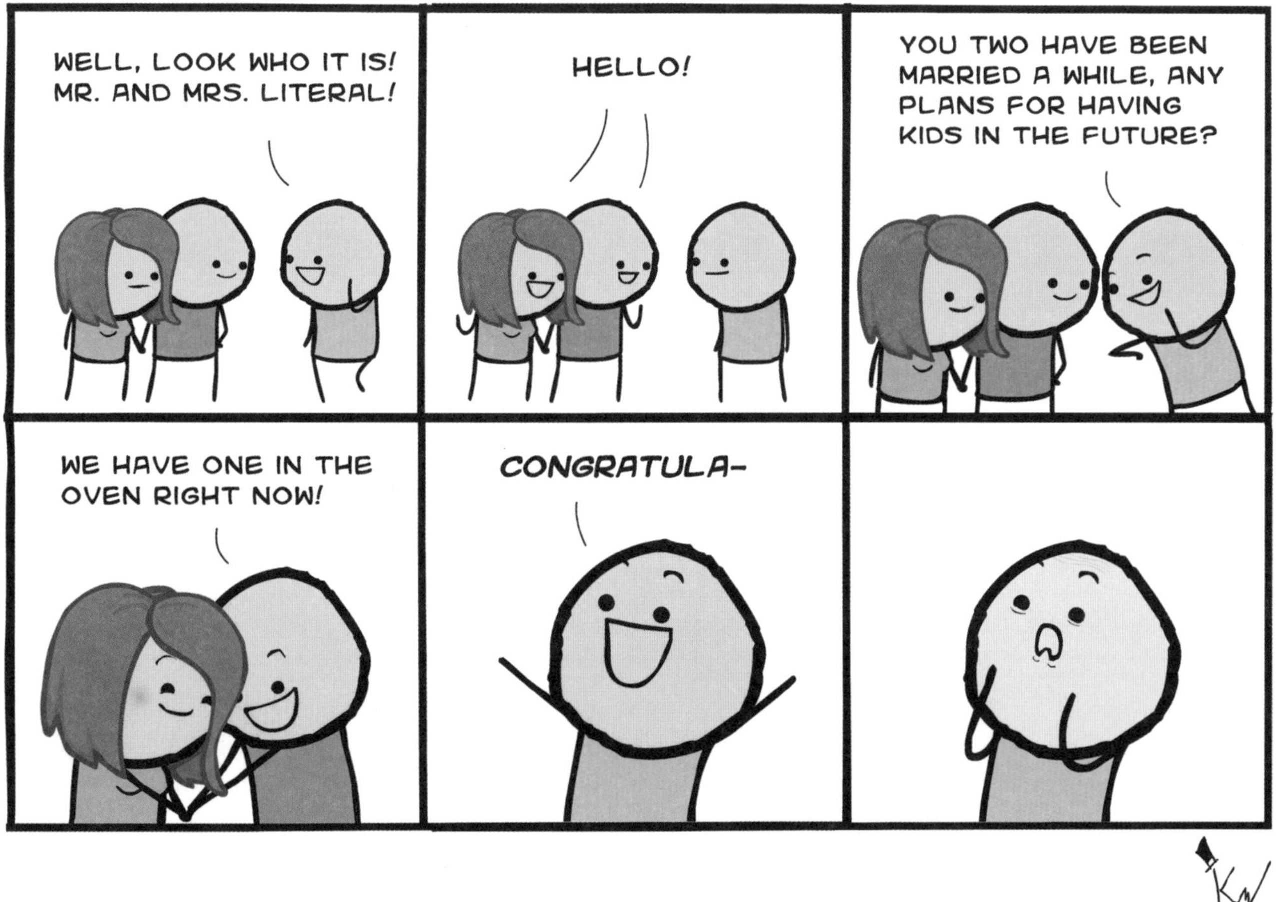
WELL, LOOK WHO IT IS! MR. AND MRS. LITERAL!
HELLO!
YOU TWO HAVE BEEN MARRIED A WHILE, ANY PLANS FOR HAVING KIDS IN THE FUTURE?
WE HAVE ONE IN THE OVEN RIGHT NOW!
CONGRATULA-
KW

WHAT DO I DO FOR A LIVING? WELL, I'M A FULL TIME MOM!
PSHH, WHO'D YOU FUCK TO GET ***THAT*** JOB?
MY HUSBAND.
OH.

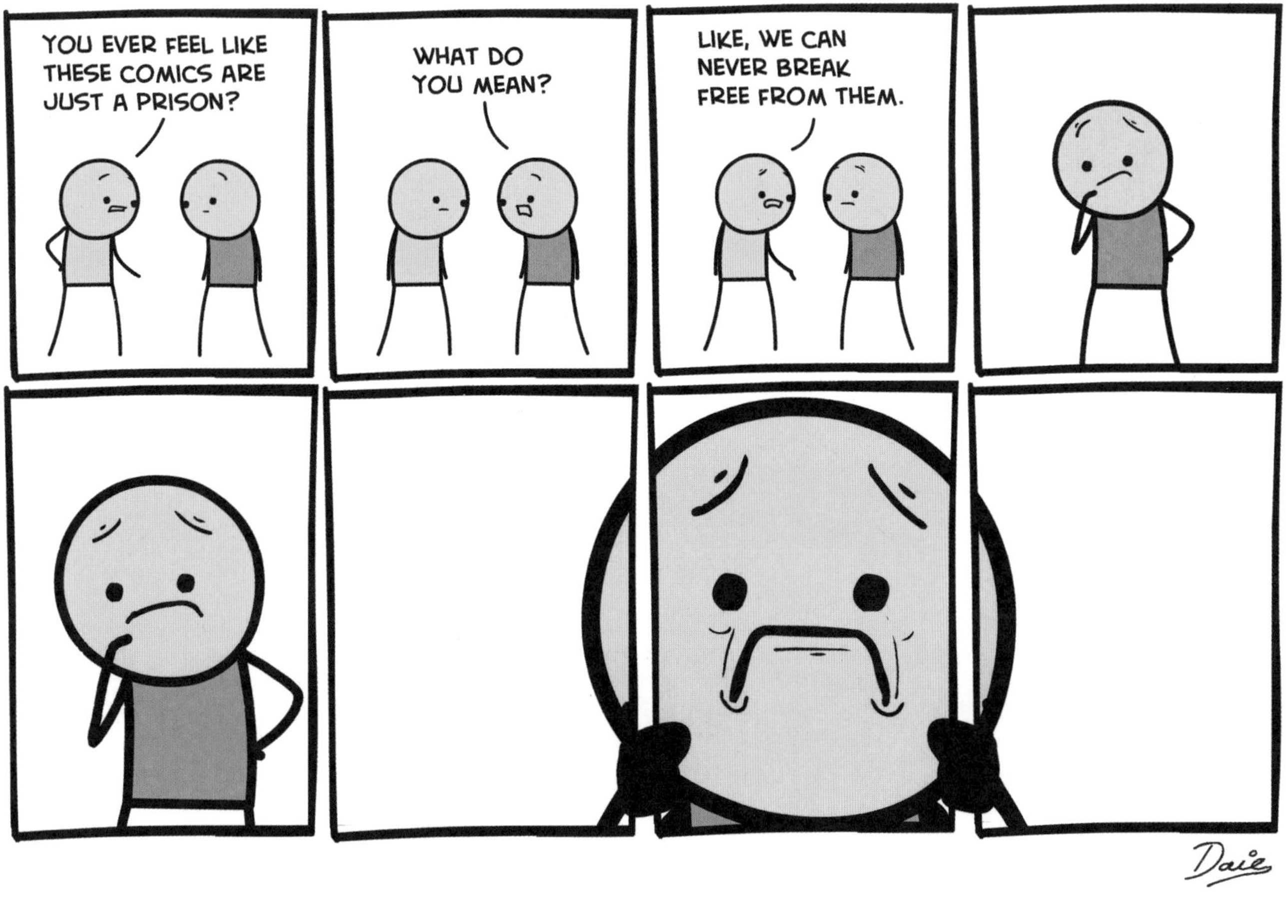
YOU EVER FEEL LIKE THESE COMICS ARE JUST A PRISON?
WHAT DO YOU MEAN?
LIKE, WE CAN NEVER BREAK FREE FROM THEM.
Dave

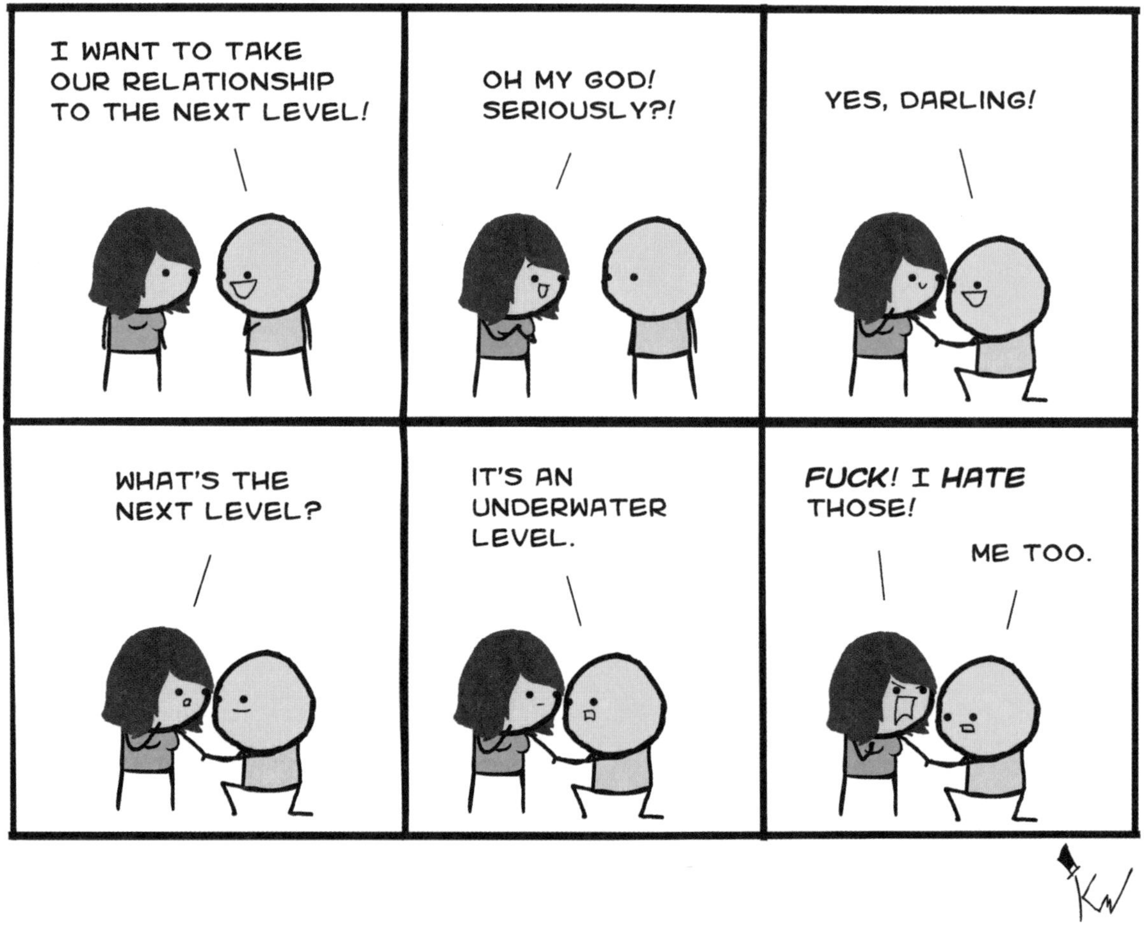
I WANT TO TAKE OUR RELATIONSHIP TO THE NEXT LEVEL!
OH MY GOD! SERIOUSLY?!
YES, DARLING!
WHAT'S THE NEXT LEVEL?
IT'S AN UNDERWATER LEVEL.
FUCK! I HATE THOSE!
ME TOO.

I COULD SURE GO FOR A PUMPKIN CARAMEL ICED LATTE RIGHT NOW.
THAT'S THE SECOND GAYEST THING YOUV'E EVER SAID.
20 SECONDS EARLIER
I'M GAY.

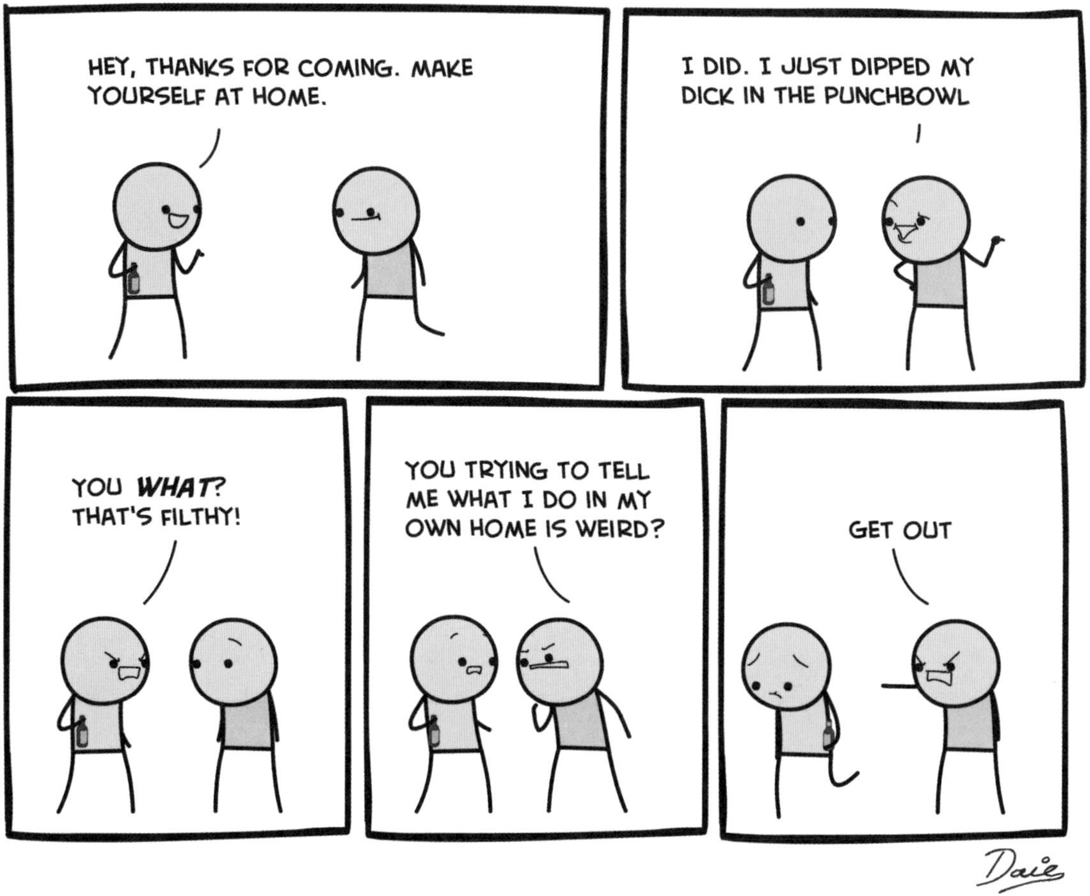
HEY, THANKS FOR COMING. MAKE YOURSELF AT HOME.
I DID. I JUST DIPPED MY DICK IN THE PUNCHBOWL
YOU **WHAT**? THAT'S FILTHY!
YOU TRYING TO TELL ME WHAT I DO IN MY OWN HOME IS WEIRD?
GET OUT
Dave

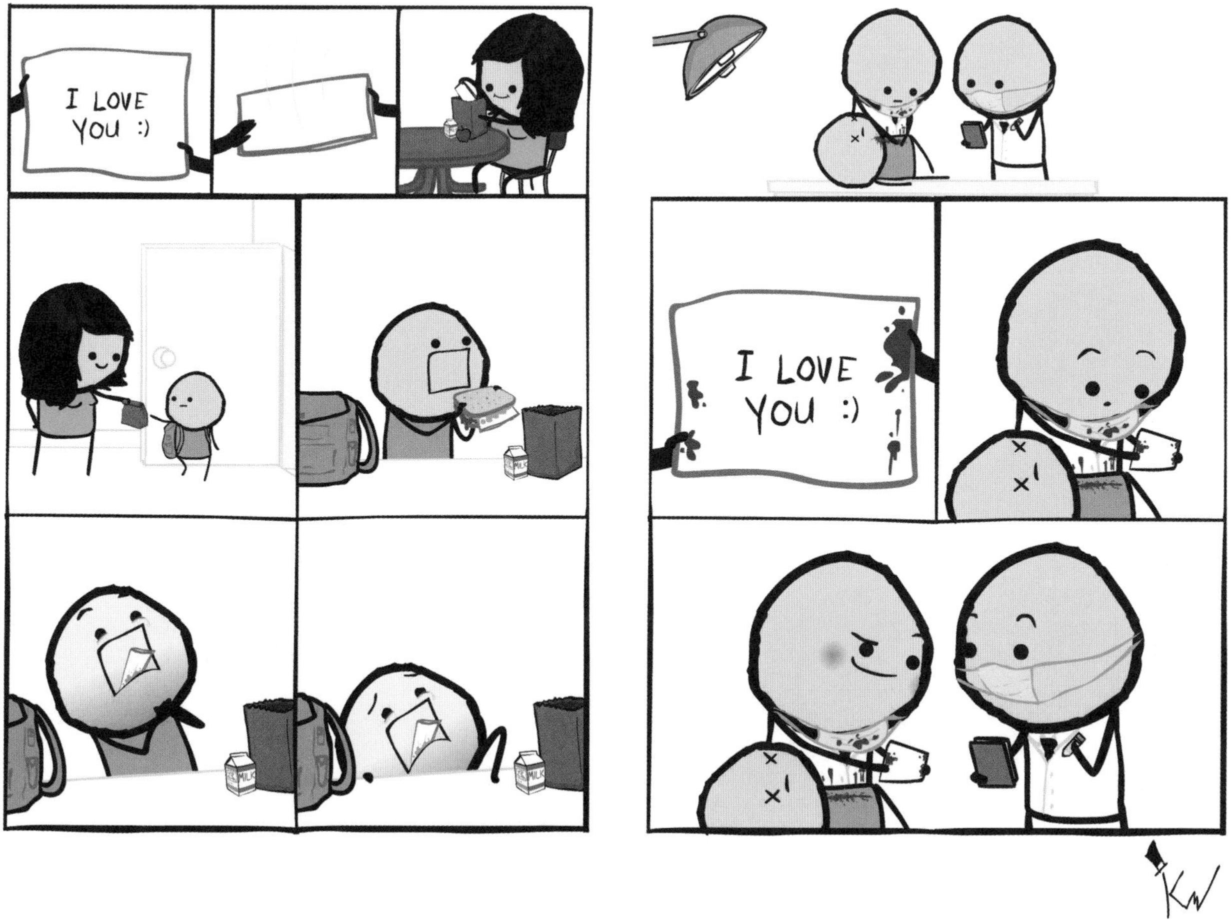
I LOVE YOU :)
MILK
MILK
MILK
I LOVE YOU :)

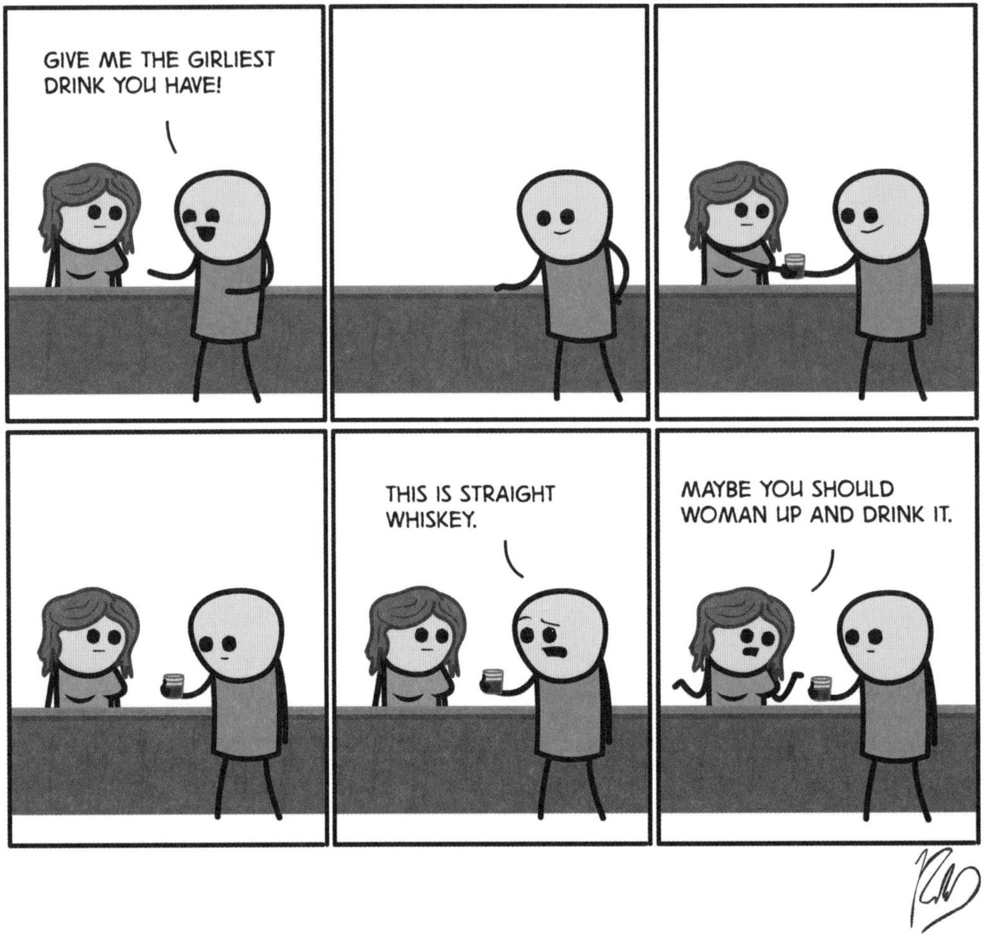
GIVE ME THE GIRLIEST DRINK YOU HAVE!
THIS IS STRAIGHT WHISKEY.
MAYBE YOU SHOULD WOMAN UP AND DRINK IT.

OKAY SON, ARE YOU READY FOR YOUR FIRST DAY OF SCHOOL? LET'S CHECK.
NOTEBOOK? CHECK. PENCILS IN PENCIL CASE? CHECK
SICK NOTE? CHECK
Dave

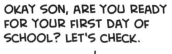

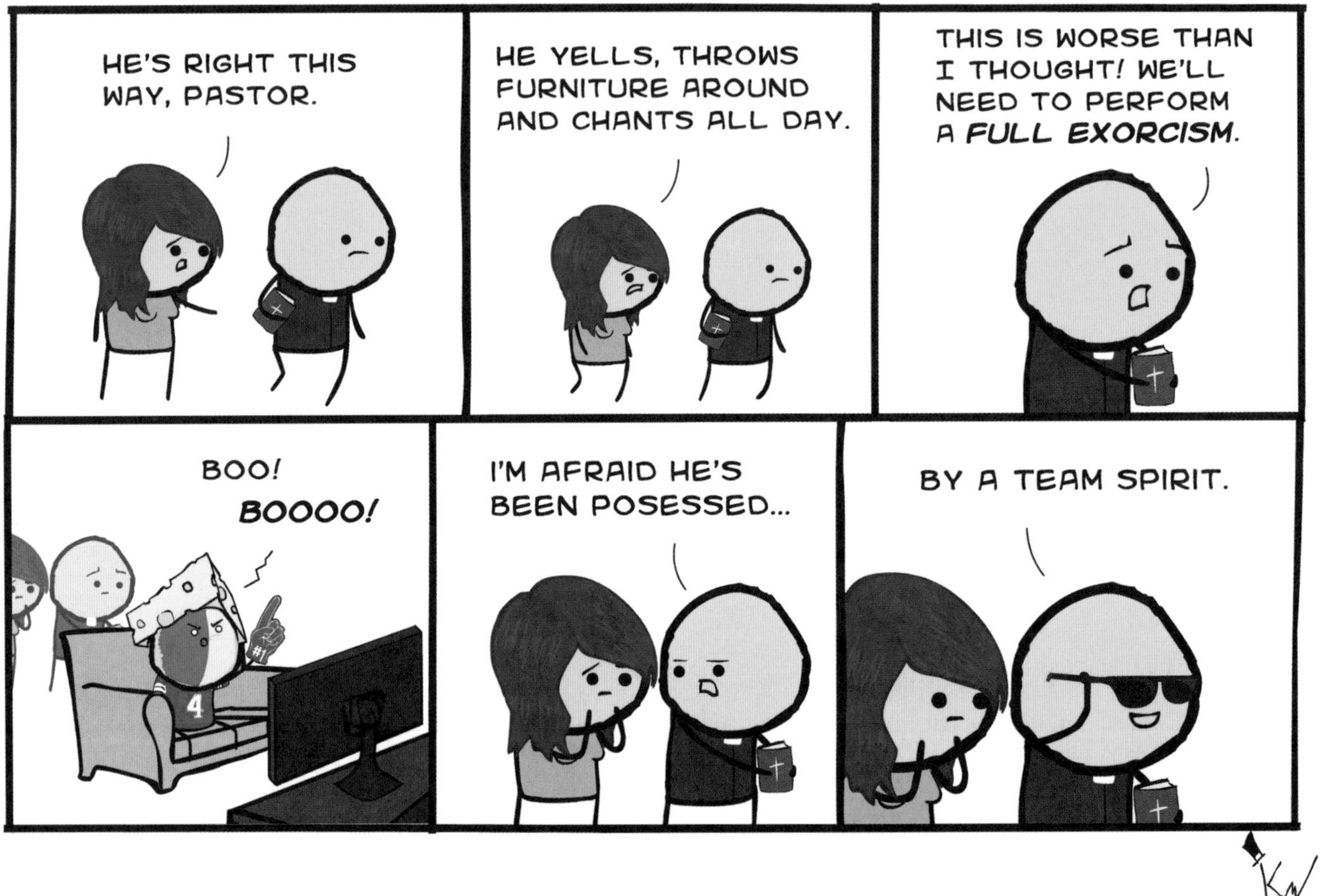
HE'S RIGHT THIS WAY, PASTOR.
HE YELLS, THROWS FURNITURE AROUND AND CHANTS ALL DAY.
THIS IS WORSE THAN I THOUGHT! WE'LL NEED TO PERFORM A **FULL EXORCISM**.
BOO!
BOOOO!
#1
4
I'M AFRAID HE'S BEEN POSESSED...
BY A TEAM SPIRIT.

THOSE WHO FAIL TO LEARN HISTORY ARE DOOMED TO REPEAT IT.
THOSE WHO FAIL TO CLEAR HISTORY ARE DOOMED TO EXPLAIN IT.

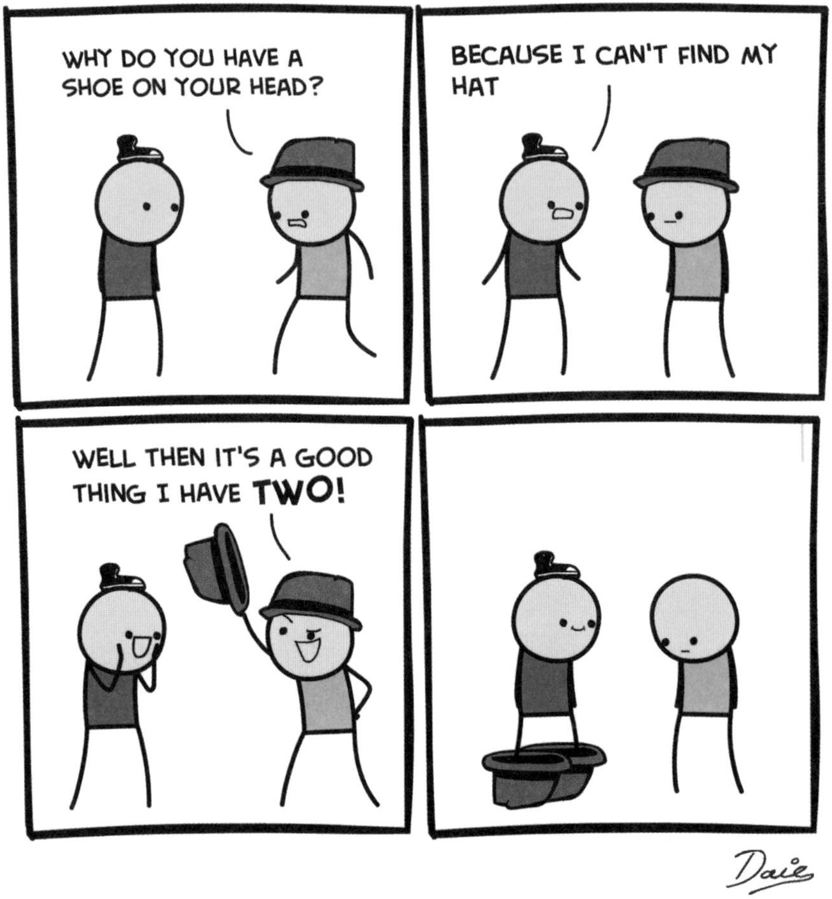
WHY DO YOU HAVE A SHOE ON YOUR HEAD?
BECAUSE I CAN'T FIND MY HAT
WELL THEN IT'S A GOOD THING I HAVE **TWO**!
Dave

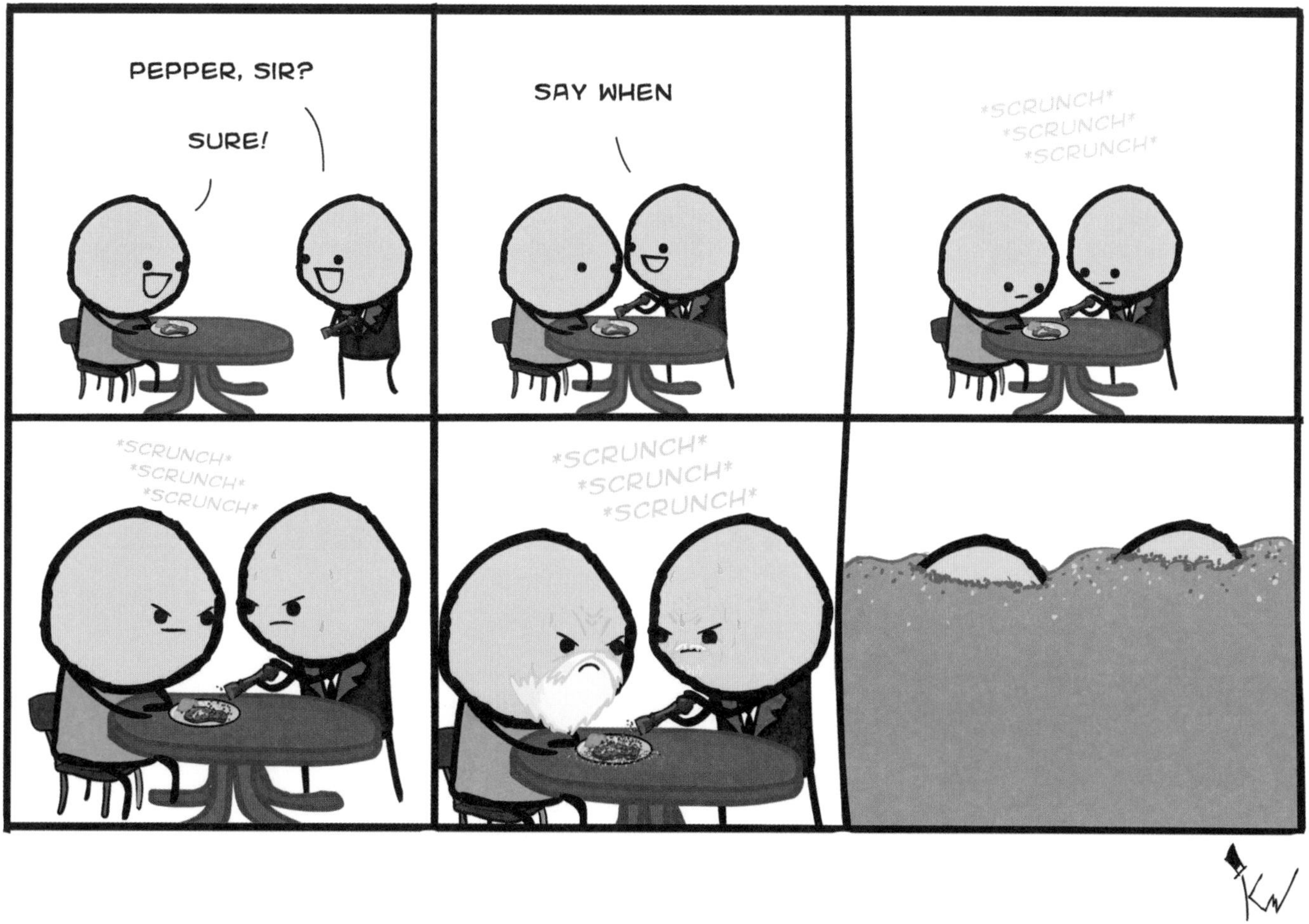
PEPPER, SIR?
SURE!
SAY WHEN
SCRUNCH
SCRUNCH
SCRUNCH
SCRUNCH
SCRUNCH
SCRUNCH
SCRUNCH
SCRUNCH
SCRUNCH

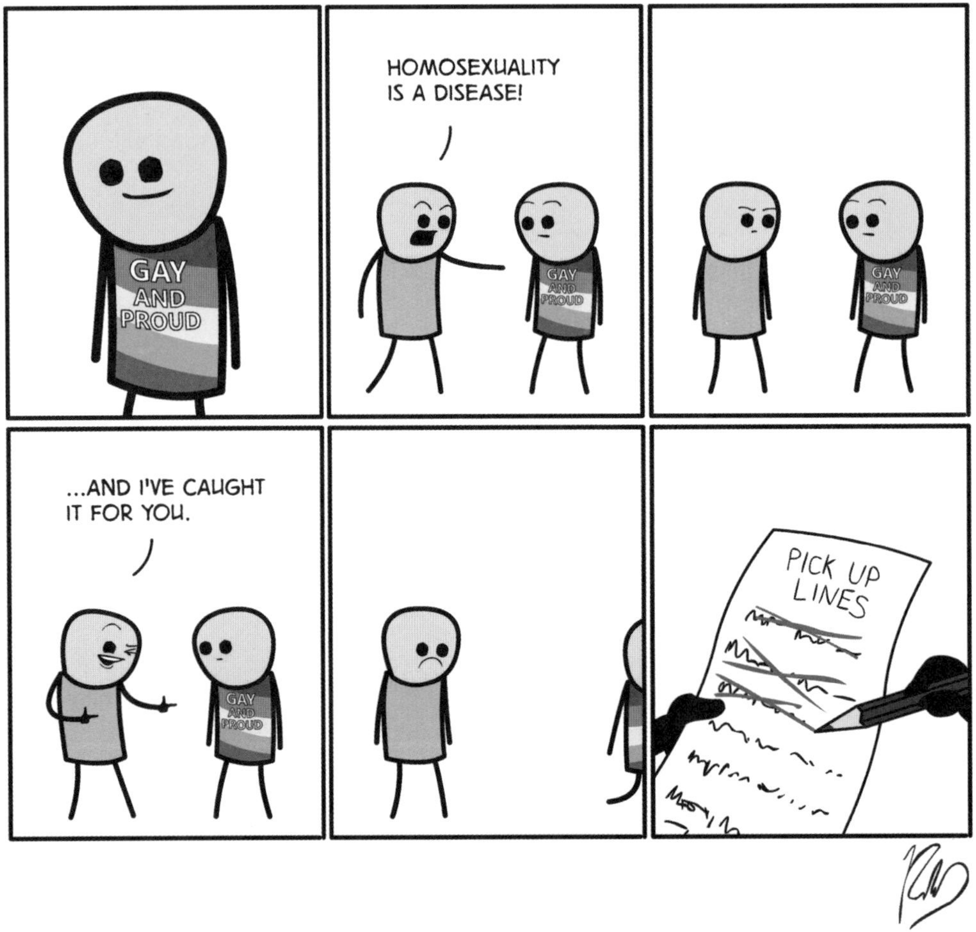
GAY AND PROUD
HOMOSEXUALITY IS A DISEASE!
GAY AND PROUD
GAY AND PROUD
GAY AND PROUD
...AND I'VE CAUGHT IT FOR YOU.
GAY AND PROUD
PICK UP LINES

HEY SOBBO, WHAT'S UP? WHY SO SAD?
I JUST GOT DIAGNOSED WITH LUNG CANCER
SLOOSH!!
THAT WASN'T MY FLOWER
Dave

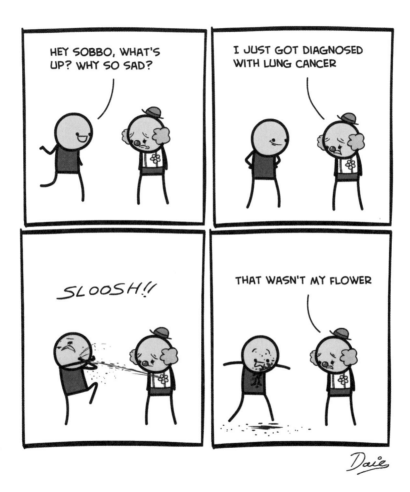

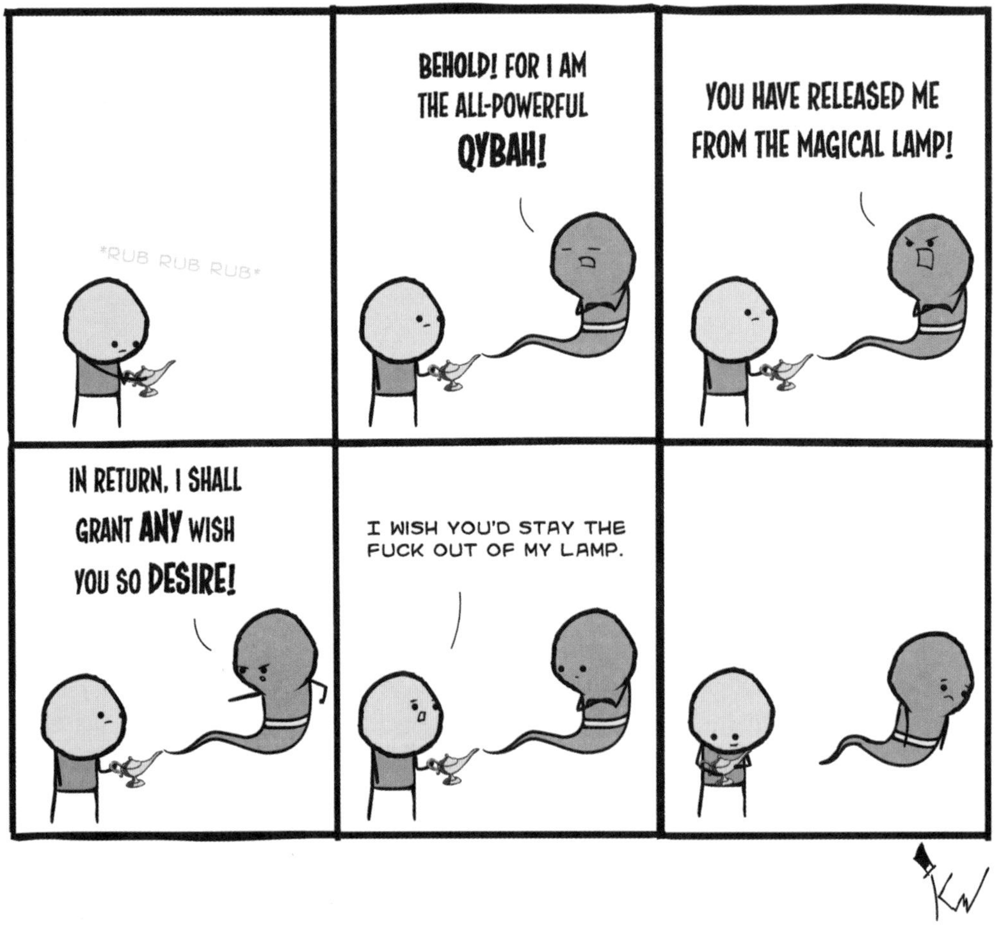
RUB RUB RUB
BEHOLD! FOR I AM THE ALL-POWERFUL QYBAH!
YOU HAVE RELEASED ME FROM THE MAGICAL LAMP!
IN RETURN, I SHALL GRANT ANY WISH YOU SO DESIRE!
I WISH YOU'D STAY THE FUCK OUT OF MY LAMP.
KW

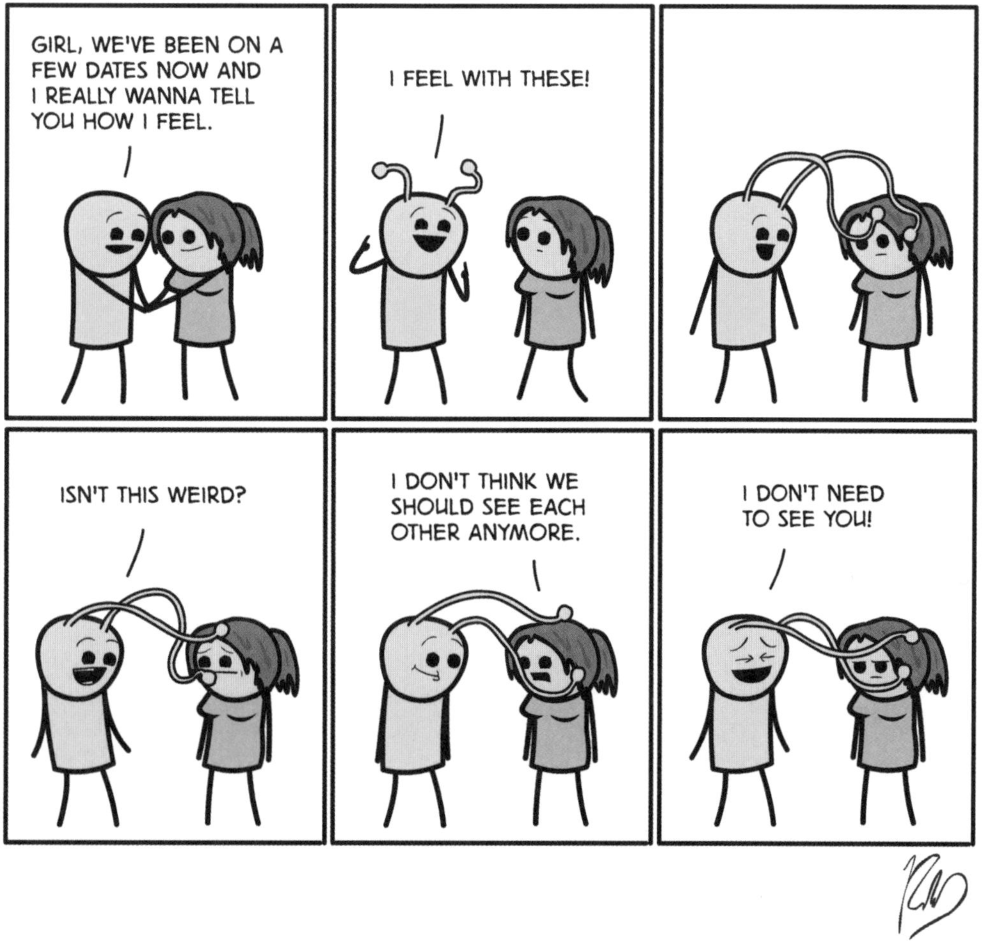
GIRL, WE'VE BEEN ON A FEW DATES NOW AND I REALLY WANNA TELL YOU HOW I FEEL.
I FEEL WITH THESE!
ISN'T THIS WEIRD?
I DON'T THINK WE SHOULD SEE EACH OTHER ANYMORE.
I DON'T NEED TO SEE YOU!

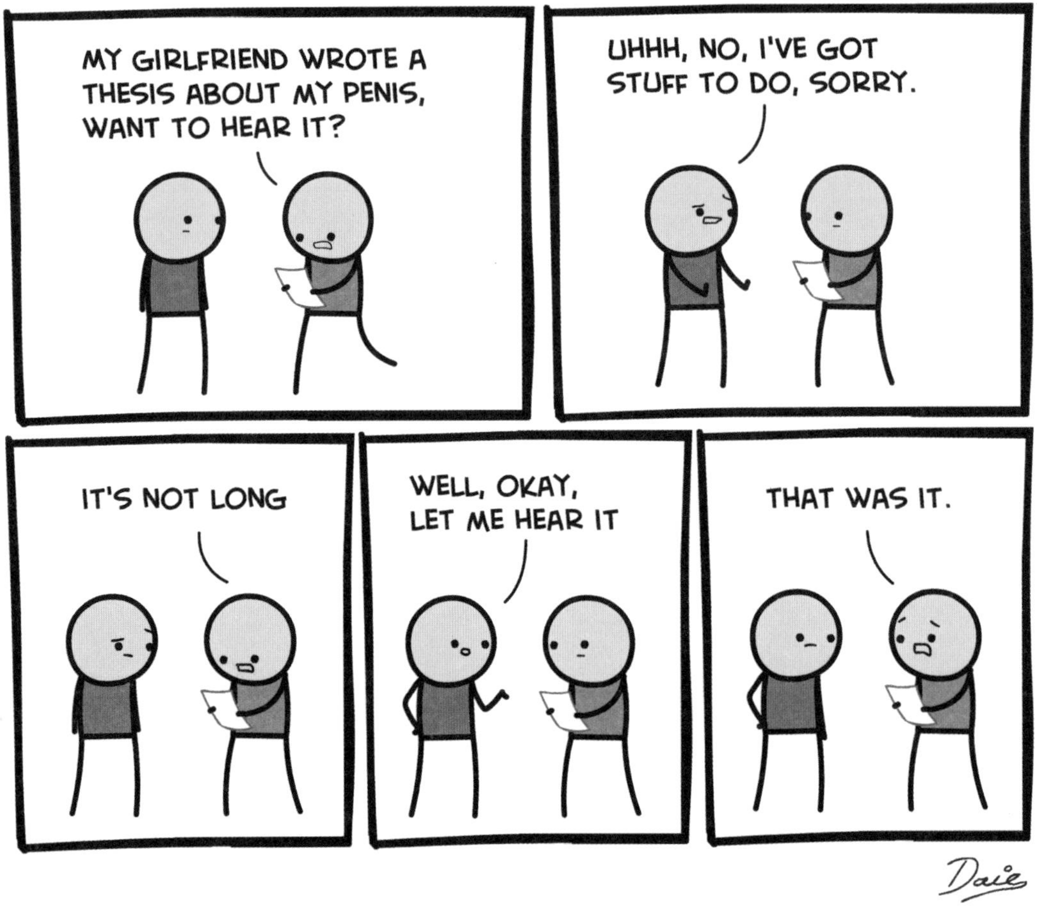
MY GIRLFRIEND WROTE A THESIS ABOUT MY PENIS, WANT TO HEAR IT?
UHHH, NO, I'VE GOT STUFF TO DO, SORRY.
IT'S NOT LONG
WELL, OKAY, LET ME HEAR IT
THAT WAS IT.
Dave

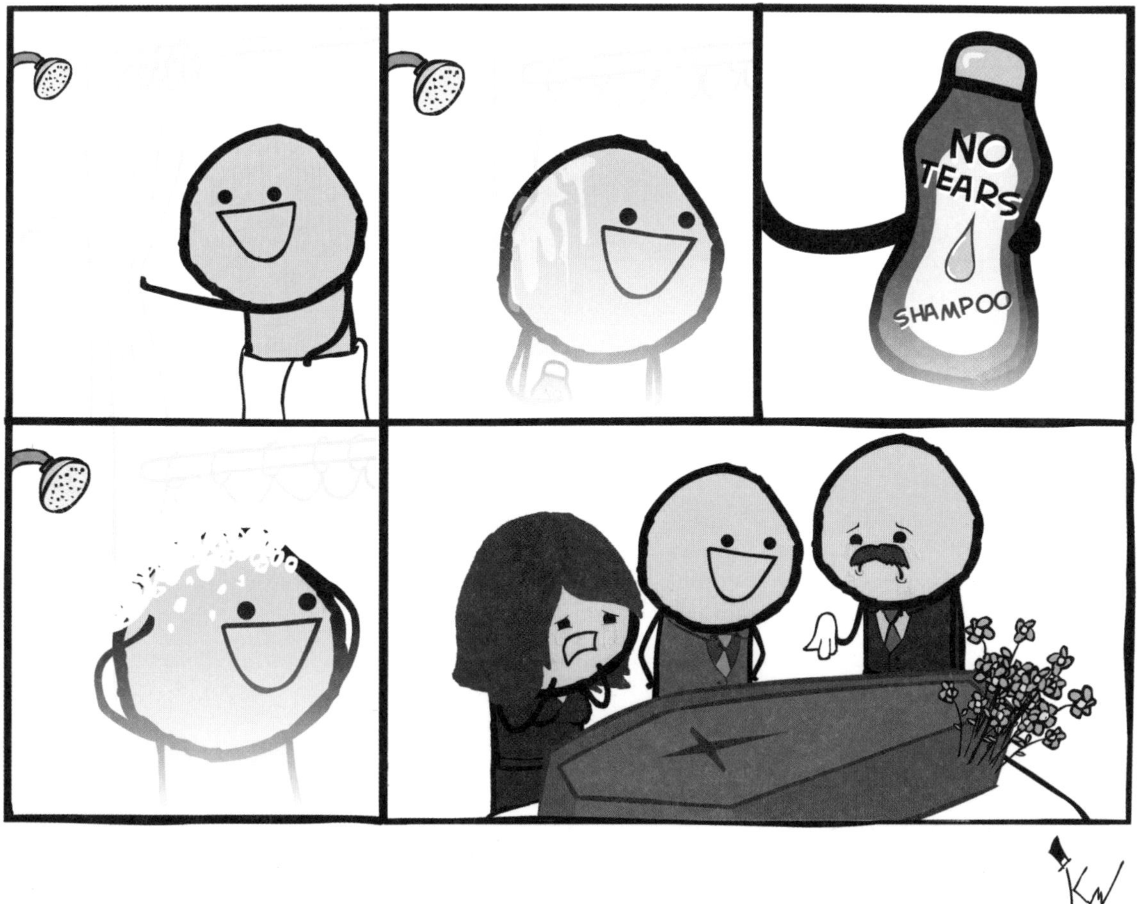
NO TEARS
SHAMPOO

SORRY I DIDN'T TEXT YOU BACK, I WAS IN A MOVIE LAST NIGHT.
I WAS IN YOUR MOM LAST NIGHT.
I WAS IN MY MOM FOR NINE MONTHS.
NICE!

DEATH, WHO TOUCHES YOU WHEN ITS YOUR TURN TO DIE?
DEATH **CAN'T** DIE, BUT IF I HAD TO...
I'D TOUCH MYSELF
Dave

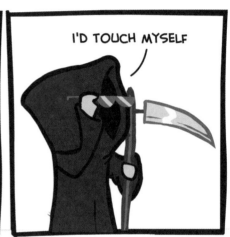

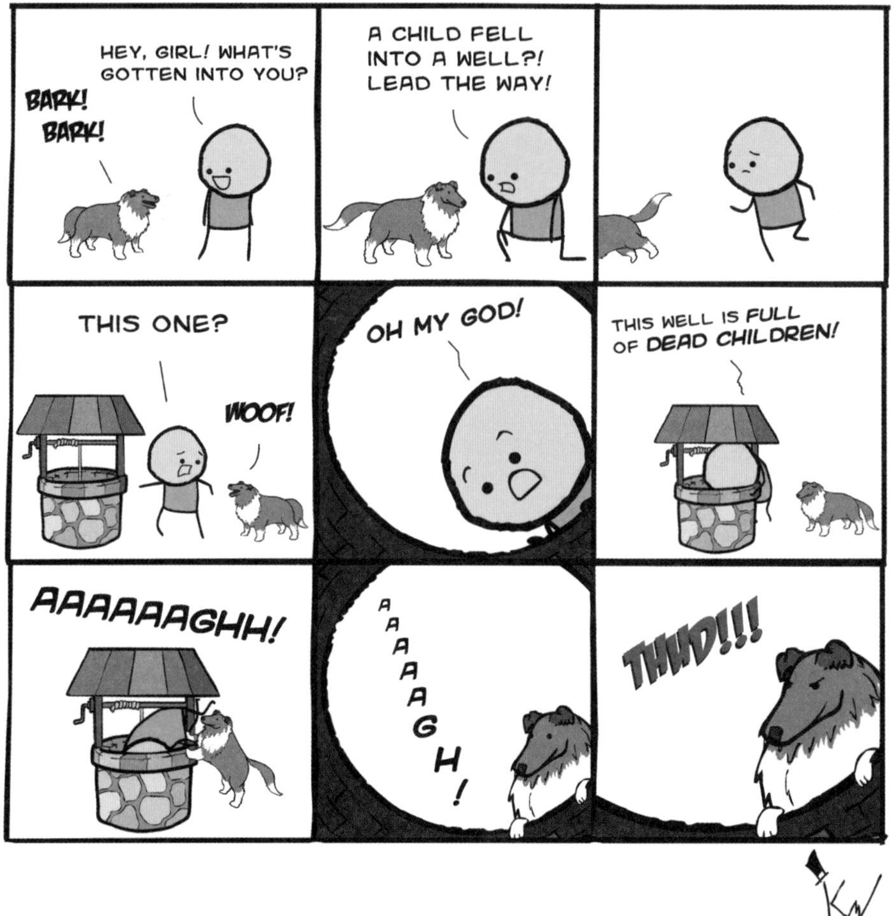
HEY, GIRL! WHAT'S GOTTEN INTO YOU?
BARK!
BARK!
A CHILD FELL INTO A WELL?! LEAD THE WAY!
THIS ONE?
WOOF!
OH MY GOD!
THIS WELL IS FULL OF DEAD CHILDREN!
AAAAAAAGHH!
AAAAAAGH!
THUD!!!

SIGH... I HATE WORKING IN SALES.
FIND THE JOB YOU LOVE, AND YOU'LL NEVER WORK A DAY IN YOUR LIFE.
AREN'T YOU UNEMPLOYED?
EXACTLY.

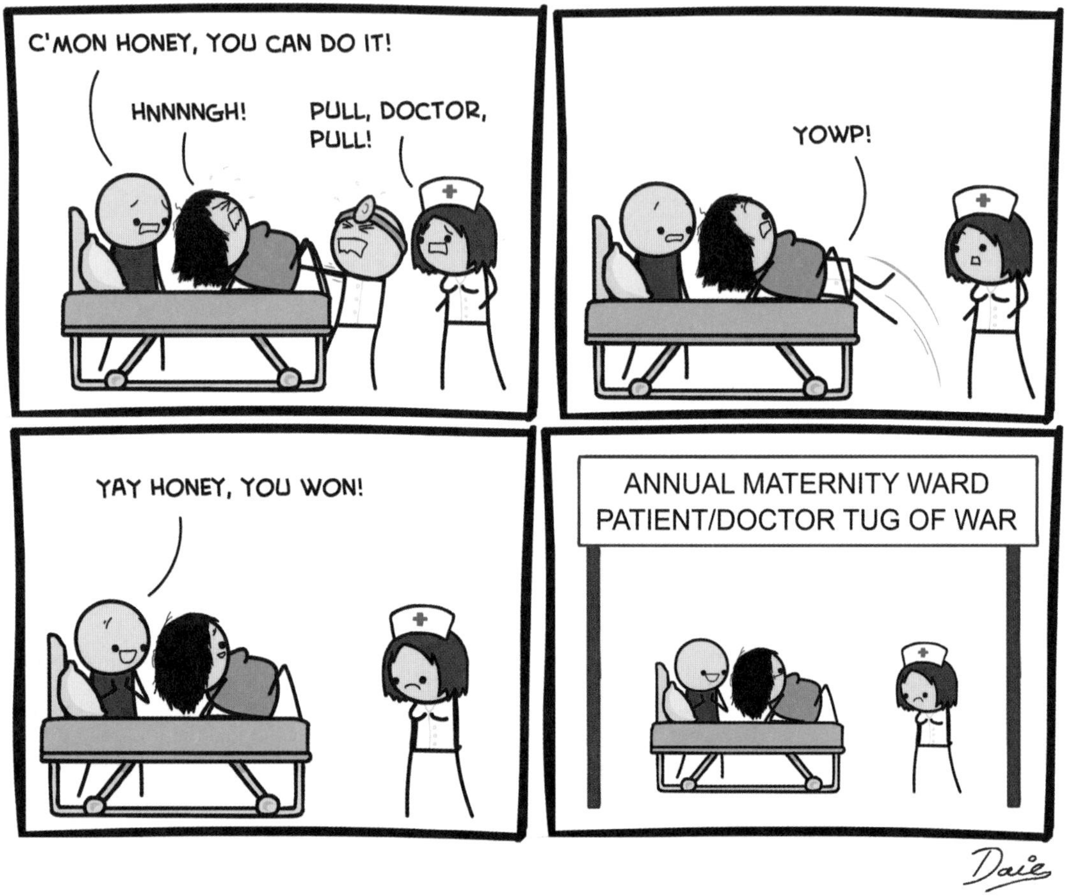
C'MON HONEY, YOU CAN DO IT!
HNNNNGH!
PULL, DOCTOR, PULL!
YOWP!
YAY HONEY, YOU WON!
ANNUAL MATERNITY WARD PATIENT/DOCTOR TUG OF WAR
Dave

ONE CUP OF JOE, PLEASE!
HERE YOU GO!
Sperm Bank
Congrats
Joe
Donor of
the Year

HONEY, IF YOU HAD TO CHOOSE, WOULD YOU RATHER I DIE OR BE FORCED TO HAVE BUTTSEX?
WELL, THE BUTTSEX OF COURSE.
AWWWWW, THAT'S NICE TO KNOW!
Dave

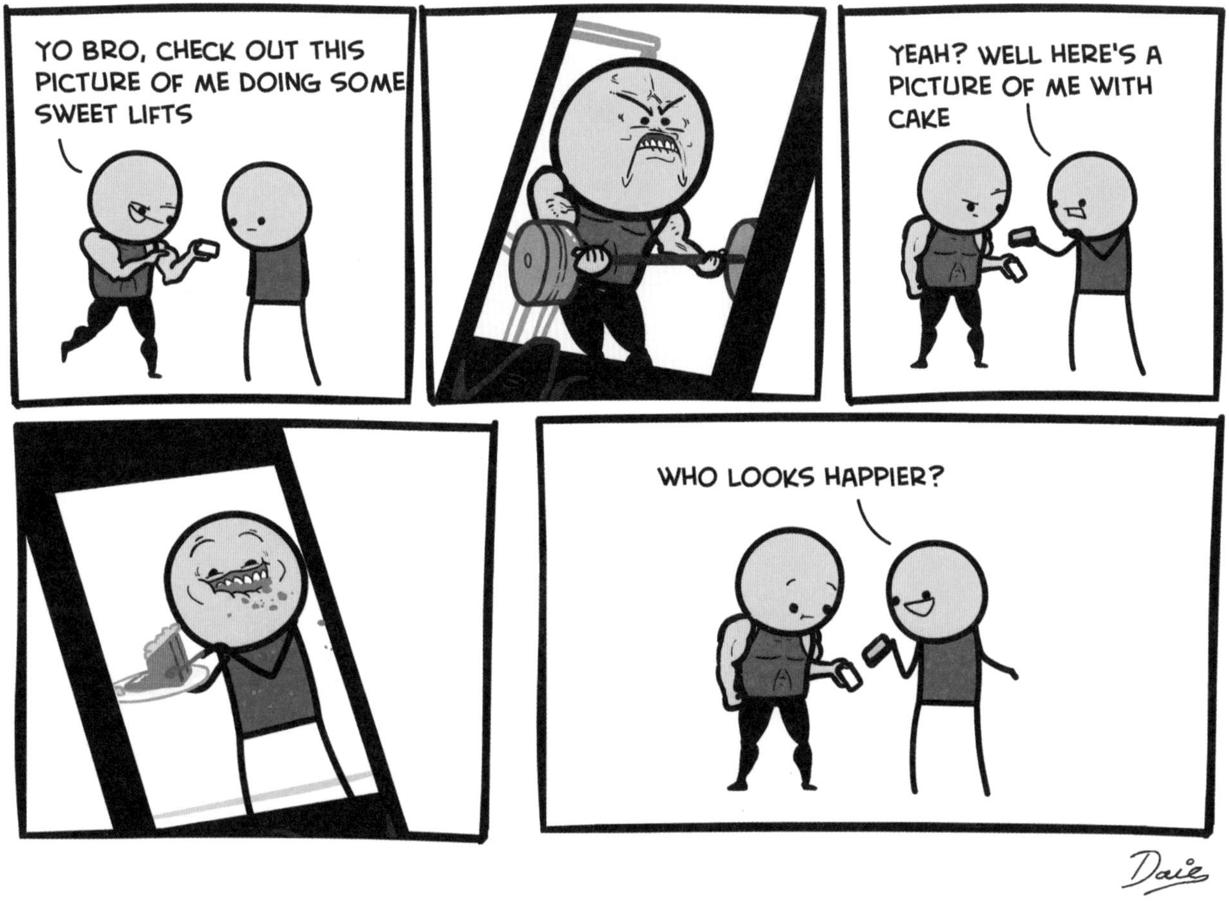
YO BRO, CHECK OUT THIS PICTURE OF ME DOING SOME SWEET LIFTS
YEAH? WELL HERE'S A PICTURE OF ME WITH CAKE
WHO LOOKS HAPPIER?
Dave

MAN, MY DAD KEEPS WALKING IN
WHILE I'M WATCHING PORN.
THAT SUCKS, DUDE.
EARLIER...
ME NEXT!
Dave

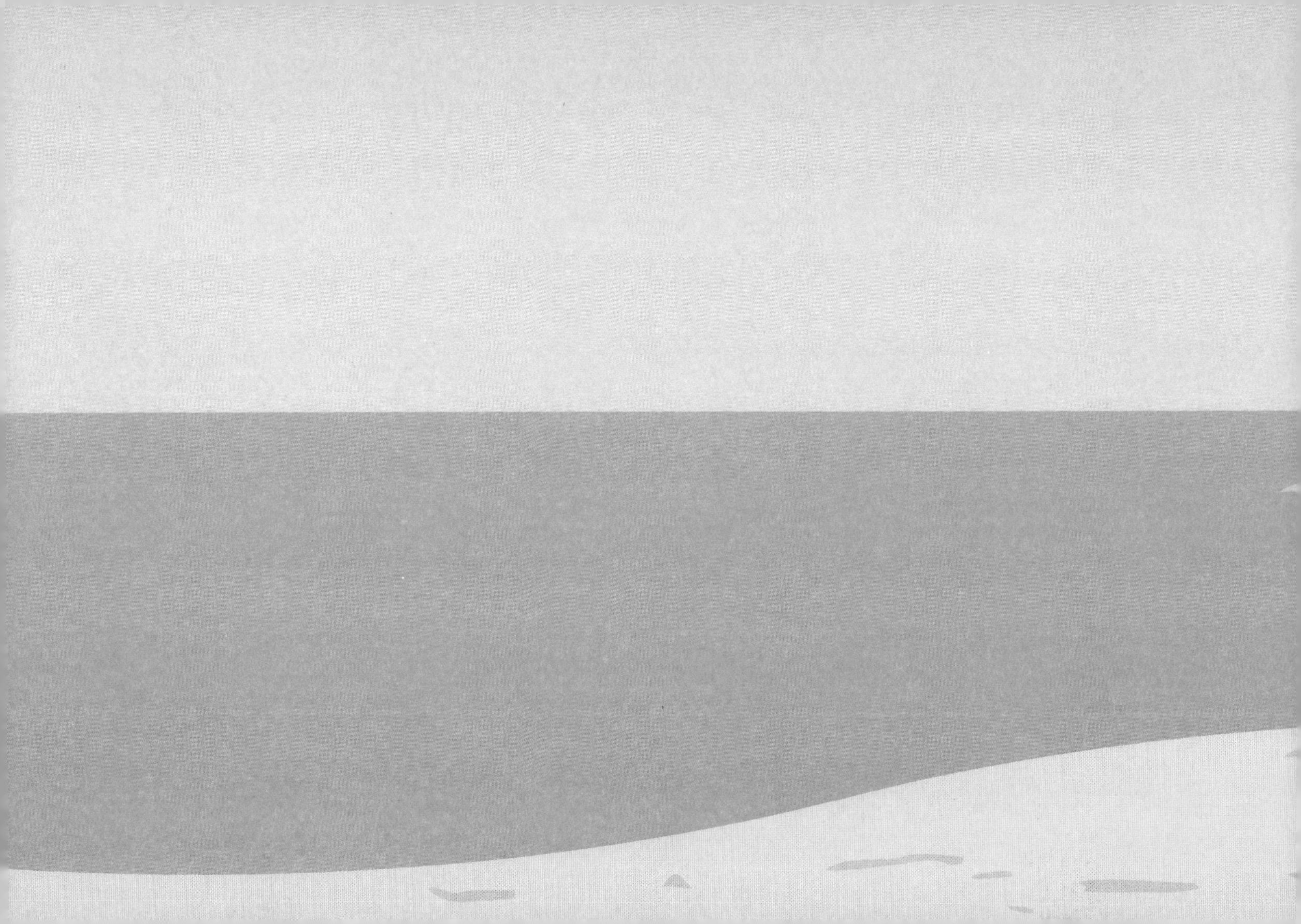

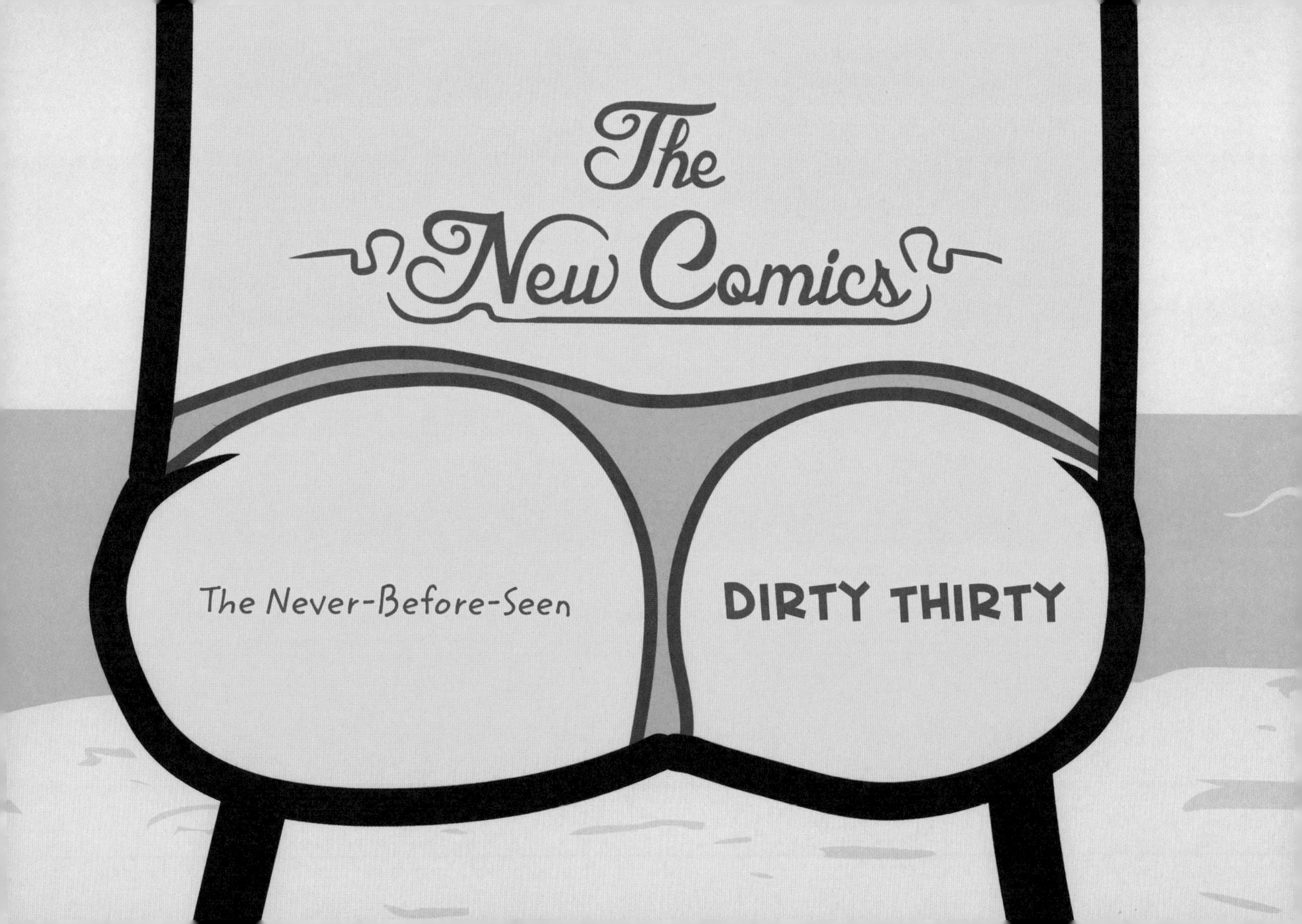
The New Comics
The Never-Before-Seen
DIRTY THIRTY

HEY JEFF. HEY CLAIRE. LONG TIME NO SEE!

YEAH, IT'S BEEN A WHILE!

HOW ARE THE KIDS?

GREAT! I'VE GOT PHOTOS OF ALL THREE OF THEM.

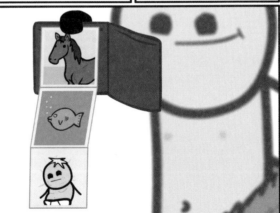

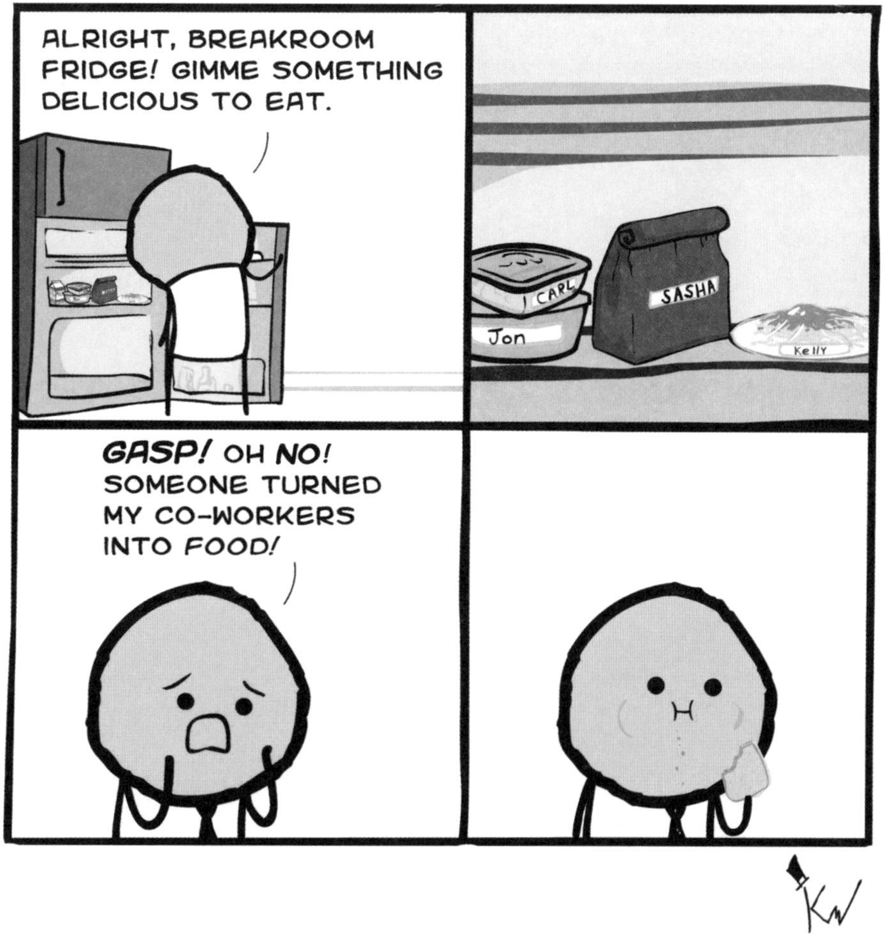
ALRIGHT, BREAKROOM FRIDGE! GIMME SOMETHING DELICIOUS TO EAT.
CARL
Jon
SASHA
Kelly
GASP! OH NO! SOMEONE TURNED MY CO-WORKERS INTO FOOD!

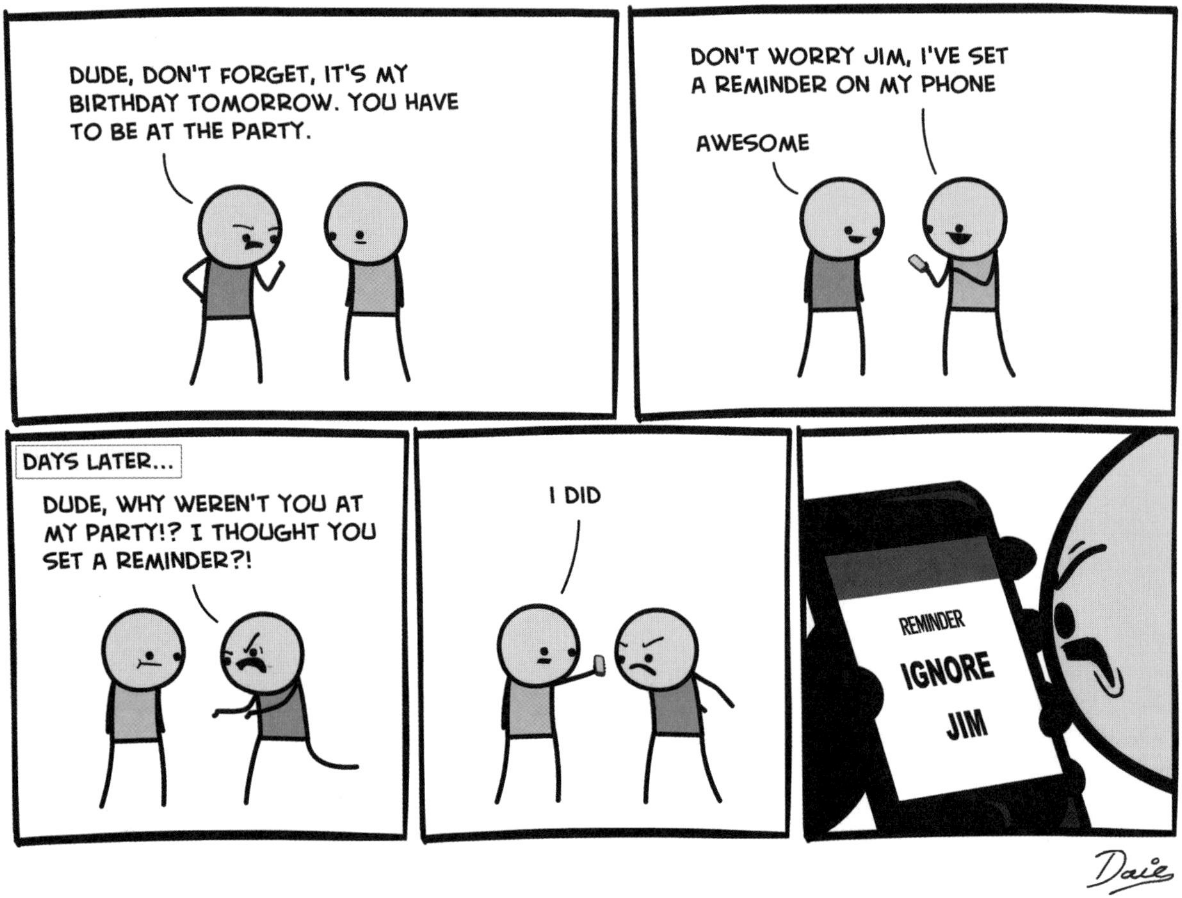
DUDE, DON'T FORGET, IT'S MY BIRTHDAY TOMORROW. YOU HAVE TO BE AT THE PARTY.
DON'T WORRY JIM, I'VE SET A REMINDER ON MY PHONE
AWESOME
DAYS LATER...
DUDE, WHY WEREN'T YOU AT MY PARTY!? I THOUGHT YOU SET A REMINDER?!
I DID
REMINDER
IGNORE
JIM
Dave

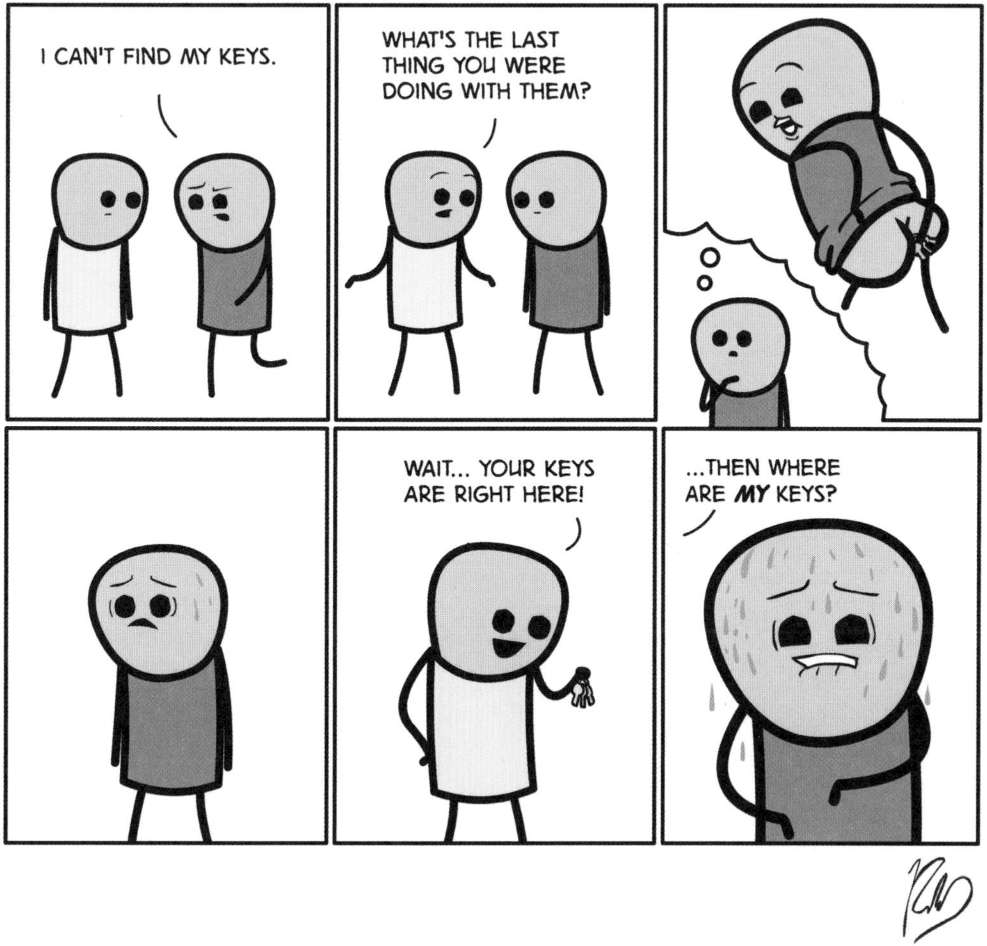
I CAN'T FIND MY KEYS.
WHAT'S THE LAST THING YOU WERE DOING WITH THEM?
WAIT... YOUR KEYS ARE RIGHT HERE!
...THEN WHERE ARE *MY* KEYS?

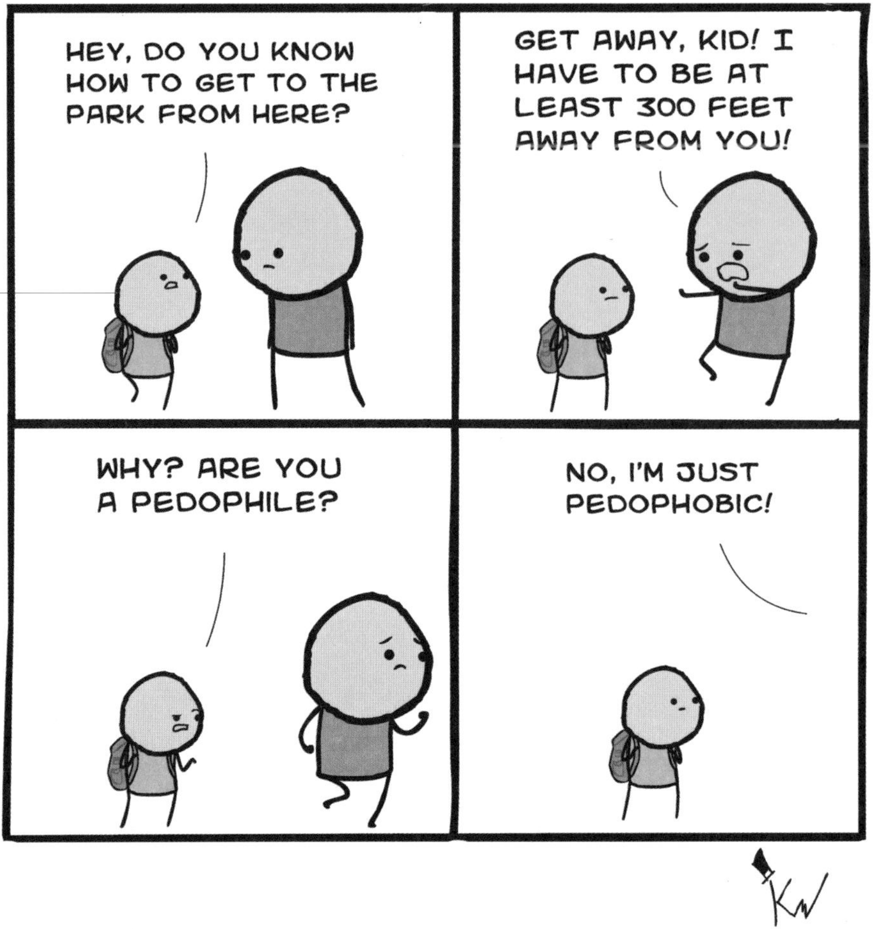
HEY, DO YOU KNOW HOW TO GET TO THE PARK FROM HERE?
GET AWAY, KID! I HAVE TO BE AT LEAST 300 FEET AWAY FROM YOU!
WHY? ARE YOU A PEDOPHILE?
NO, I'M JUST PEDOPHOBIC!
KW

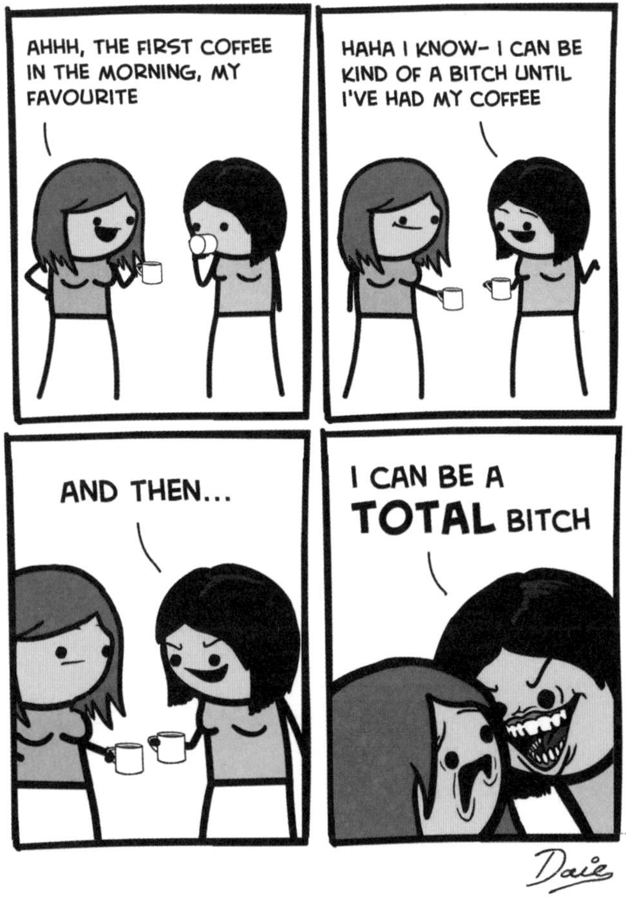
AHHH, THE FIRST COFFEE IN THE MORNING, MY FAVOURITE
HAHA I KNOW- I CAN BE KIND OF A BITCH UNTIL I'VE HAD MY COFFEE
AND THEN...
I CAN BE A TOTAL BITCH
Dave

WANNA DO A FAST AND FURIOUS MARATHON AT MY PLACE TONIGHT?
SURE... I'LL BRING THE POPCORN!
Later.
OH JEEZ... WHOOPS!
I GUESS WE *BOTH* BROUGHT POPCORN.

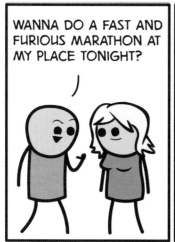

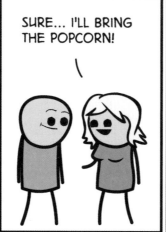

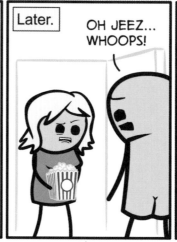

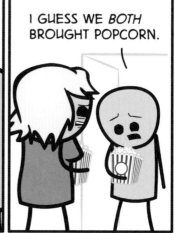

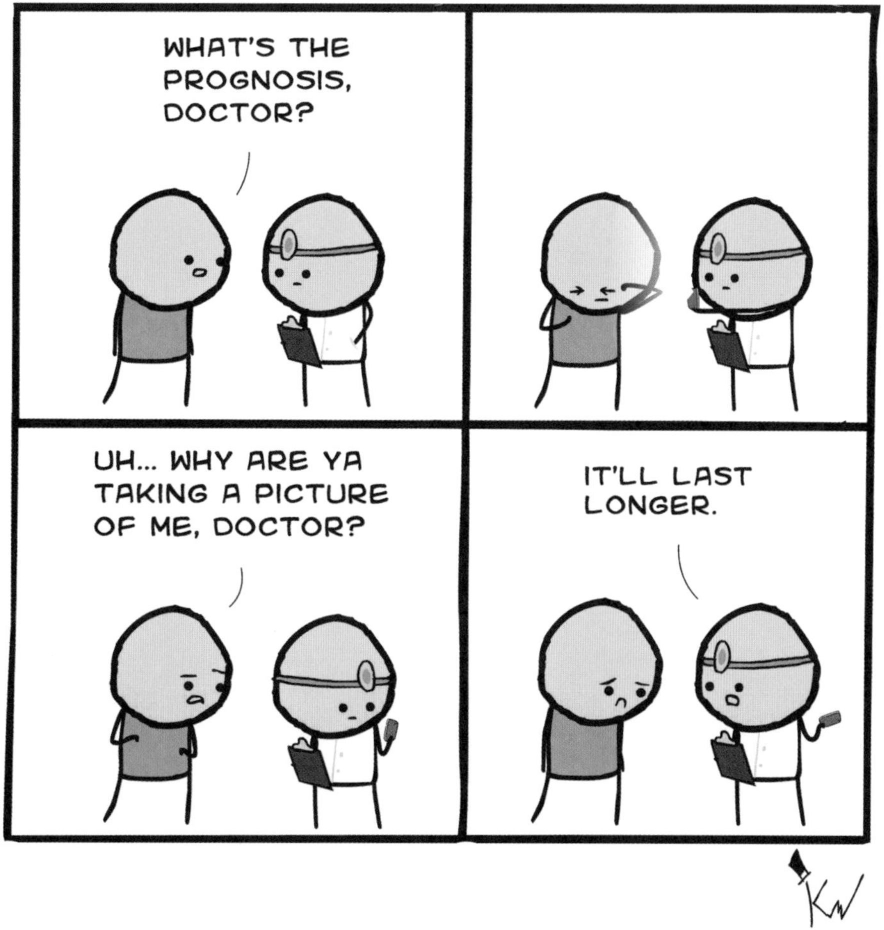
WHAT'S THE PROGNOSIS, DOCTOR?
UH... WHY ARE YA TAKING A PICTURE OF ME, DOCTOR?
IT'LL LAST LONGER.

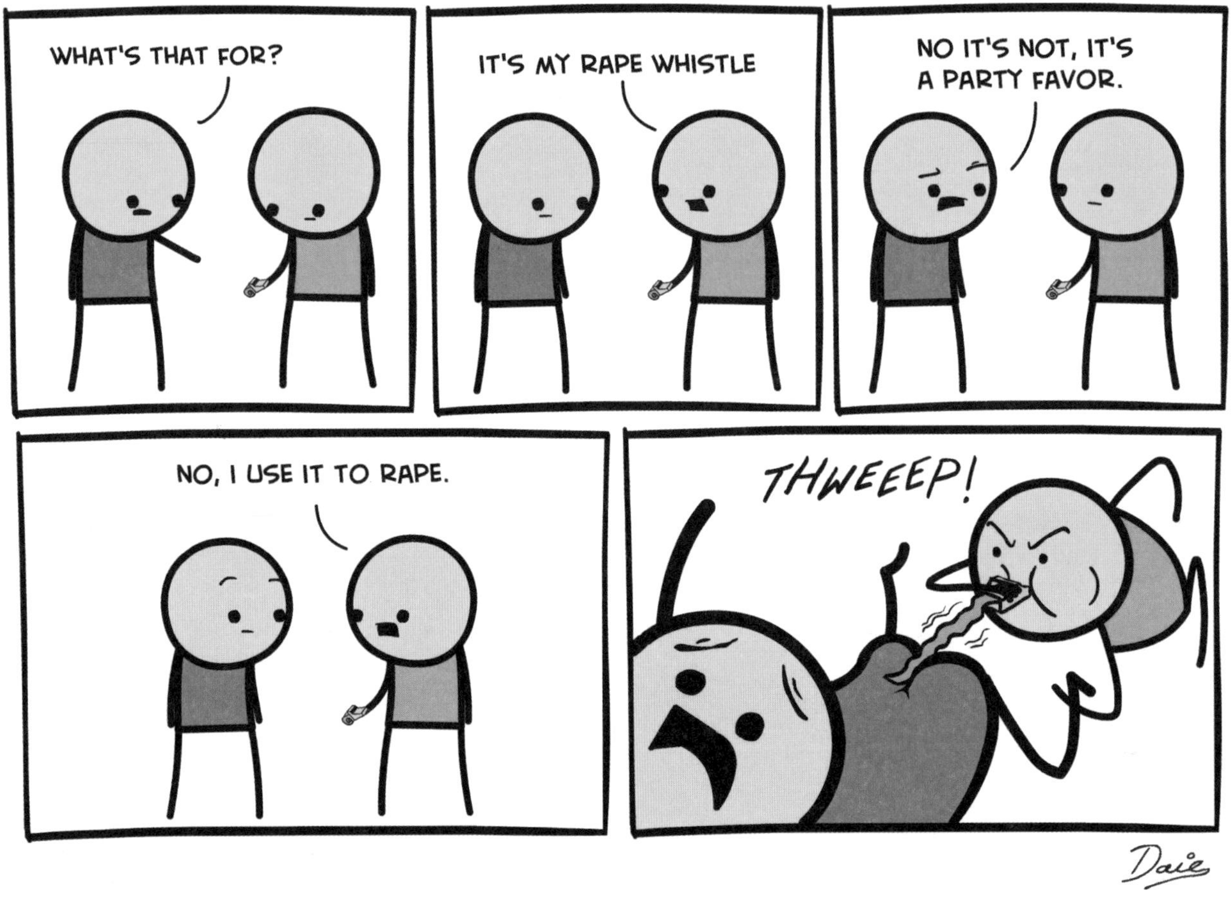
WHAT'S THAT FOR?
IT'S MY RAPE WHISTLE
NO IT'S NOT, IT'S A PARTY FAVOR.
NO, I USE IT TO RAPE.
THWEEEP!
Dave

YOU STAND ACCUSED OF BURNING DOWN TWO DAYCARES AND MURDERING ELEVEN ELDERLY WOMEN WITH YOUR CAR.
DO YOU HAVE ANYTHING TO SAY IN YOUR DEFENSE?
I HADN'T HAD MY CUP OF COFFEE YET.
YOU'RE FREE TO GO.

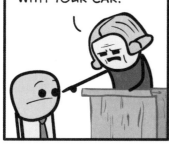

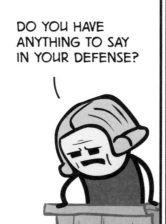

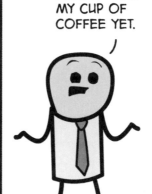

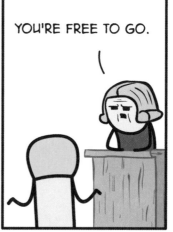

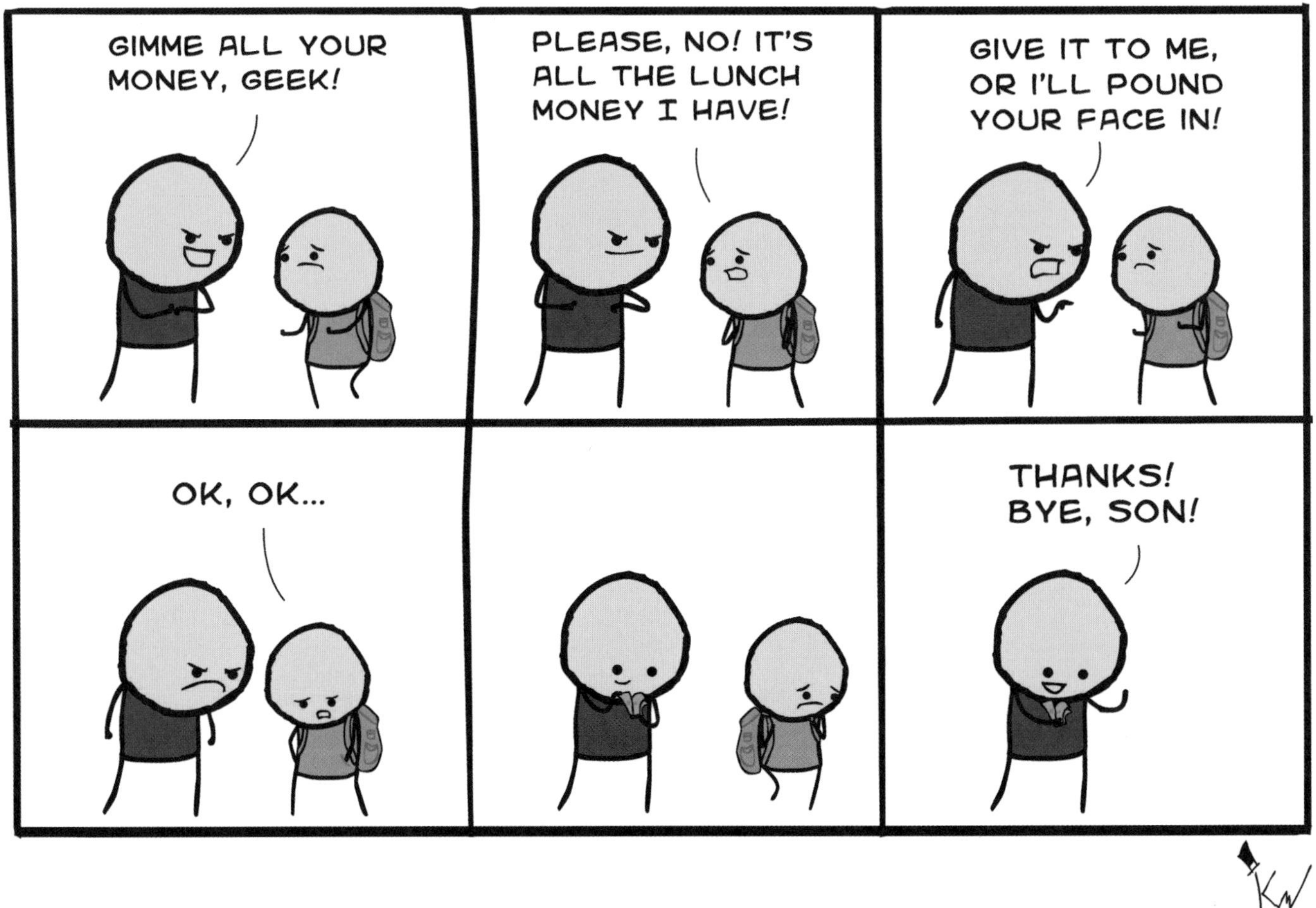
GIMME ALL YOUR MONEY, GEEK!
PLEASE, NO! IT'S ALL THE LUNCH MONEY I HAVE!
GIVE IT TO ME, OR I'LL POUND YOUR FACE IN!
OK, OK...
THANKS! BYE, SON!

MODERN SKYSCRAPERS ARE JUST PHALLIC SHAPES THAT SYMBOLISE MALE DOMINANCE!
AS A FEMINIST I FIND THIS VERY OBJECTIONABLE.
O-OK. WHAT CAN WE DO TO FIX IT?
30 YEARS LATER...
Dave

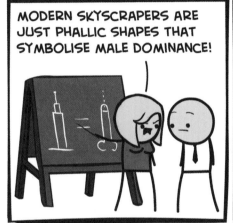

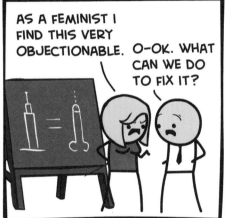

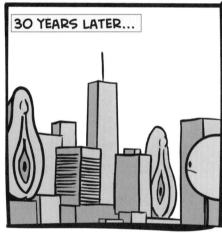

JUST ONCE, I WANT YOU TO STOP MAKING JOKES. I'M SERIOUS!
HELLO, SERIOUS. MY NAME'S DAD.
DAD! I'M PREGNANT!
HAVE YOU SEEN SERIOUS AROUND? SHE WAS JUST HERE!

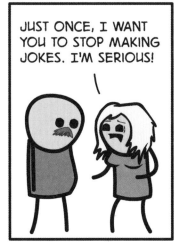

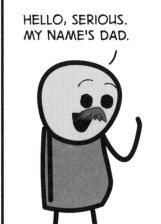

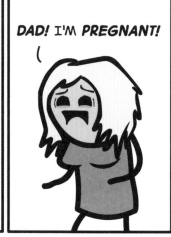

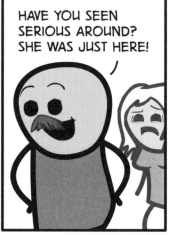

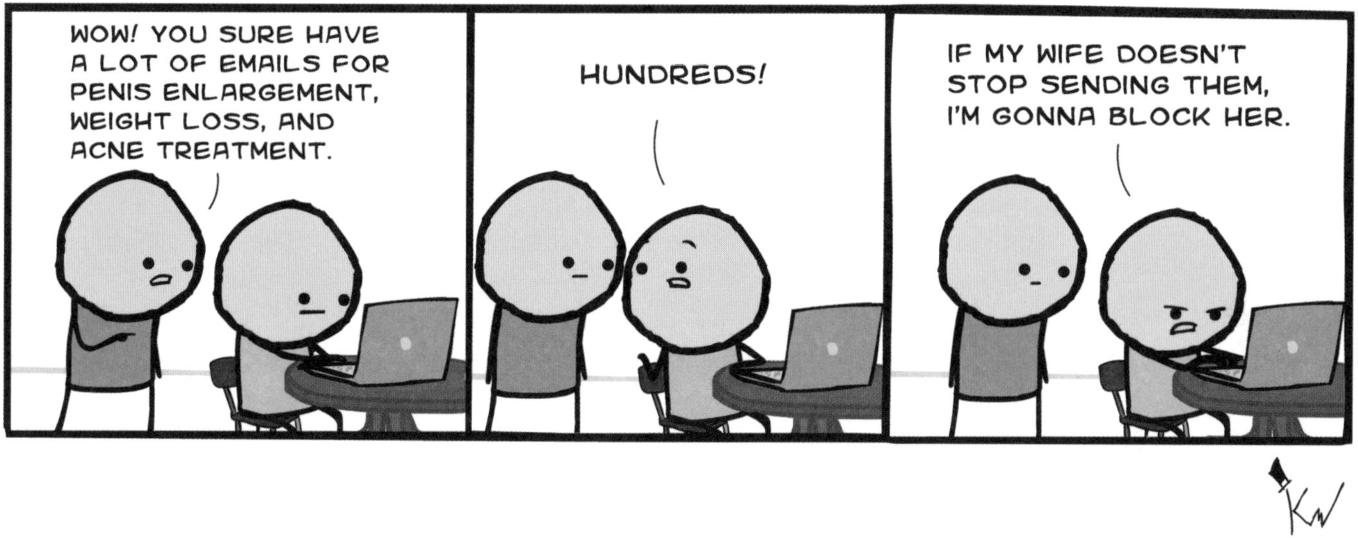
WOW! YOU SURE HAVE A LOT OF EMAILS FOR PENIS ENLARGEMENT, WEIGHT LOSS, AND ACNE TREATMENT.
HUNDREDS!
IF MY WIFE DOESN'T STOP SENDING THEM, I'M GONNA BLOCK HER.
KW

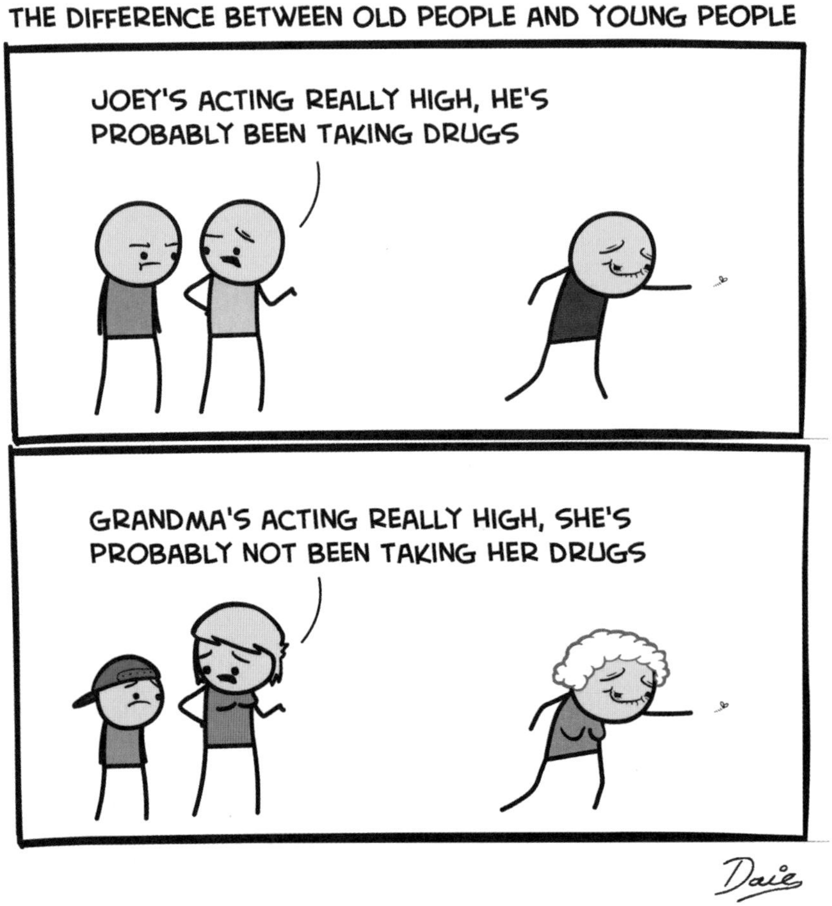
THE DIFFERENCE BETWEEN OLD PEOPLE AND YOUNG PEOPLE
JOEY'S ACTING REALLY HIGH, HE'S PROBABLY BEEN TAKING DRUGS
GRANDMA'S ACTING REALLY HIGH, SHE'S PROBABLY NOT BEEN TAKING HER DRUGS
Dave

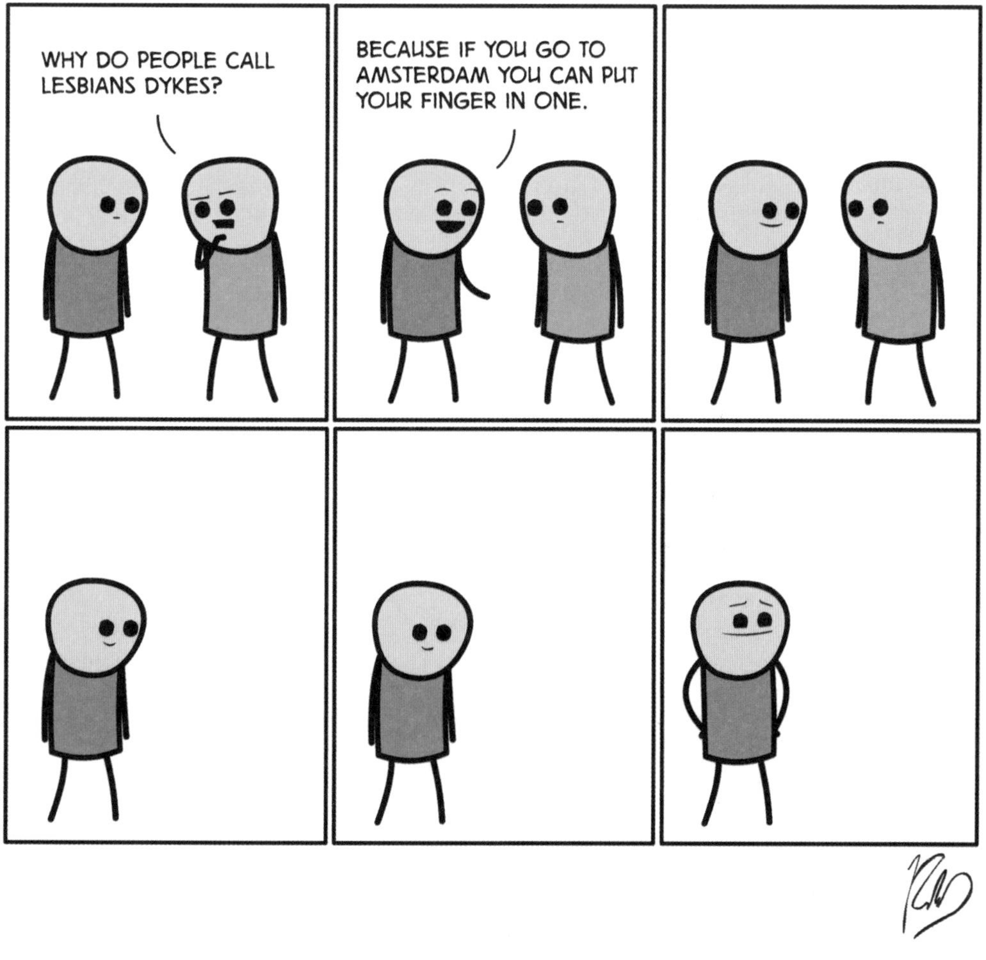
WHY DO PEOPLE CALL LESBIANS DYKES?
BECAUSE IF YOU GO TO AMSTERDAM YOU CAN PUT YOUR FINGER IN ONE.

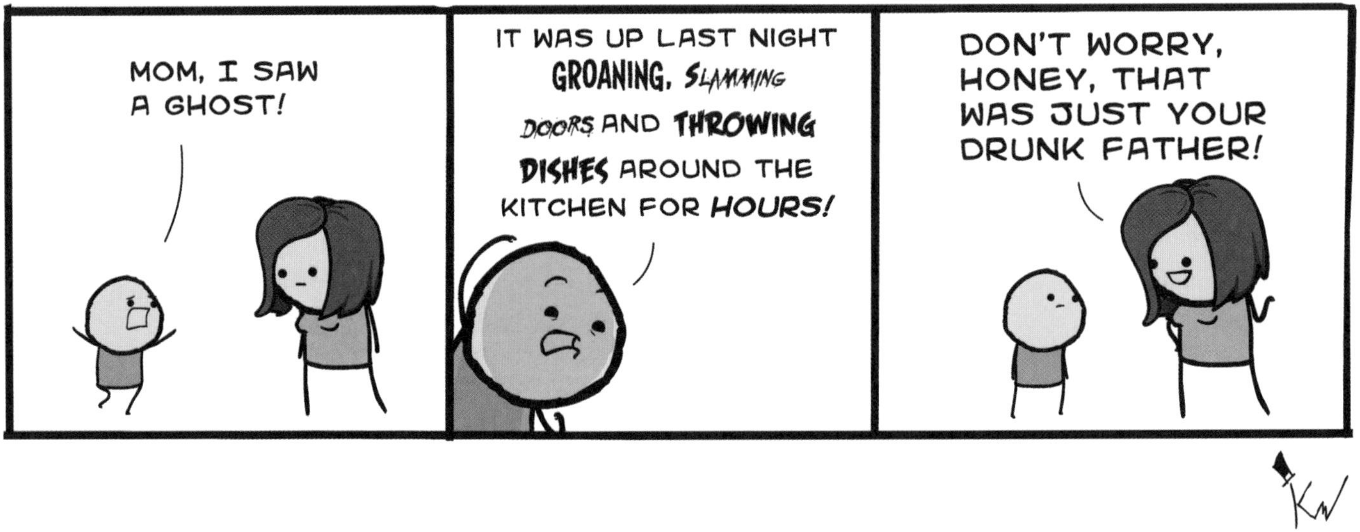
MOM, I SAW A GHOST!
IT WAS UP LAST NIGHT GROANING, SLAMMING DOORS AND THROWING DISHES AROUND THE KITCHEN FOR HOURS!
DON'T WORRY, HONEY, THAT WAS JUST YOUR DRUNK FATHER!
KW

OKAY SON, BE SAD FOR THE CAMERA!
SAD? DON'T YOU MEAN HAPPY? WHY SAD?
BECAUSE IT'S RAN OUT OF BATTERIES
Dave

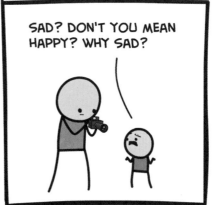

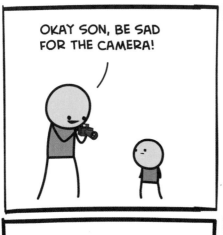

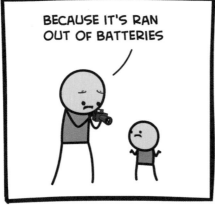

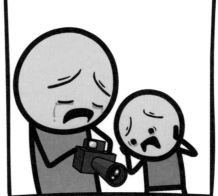

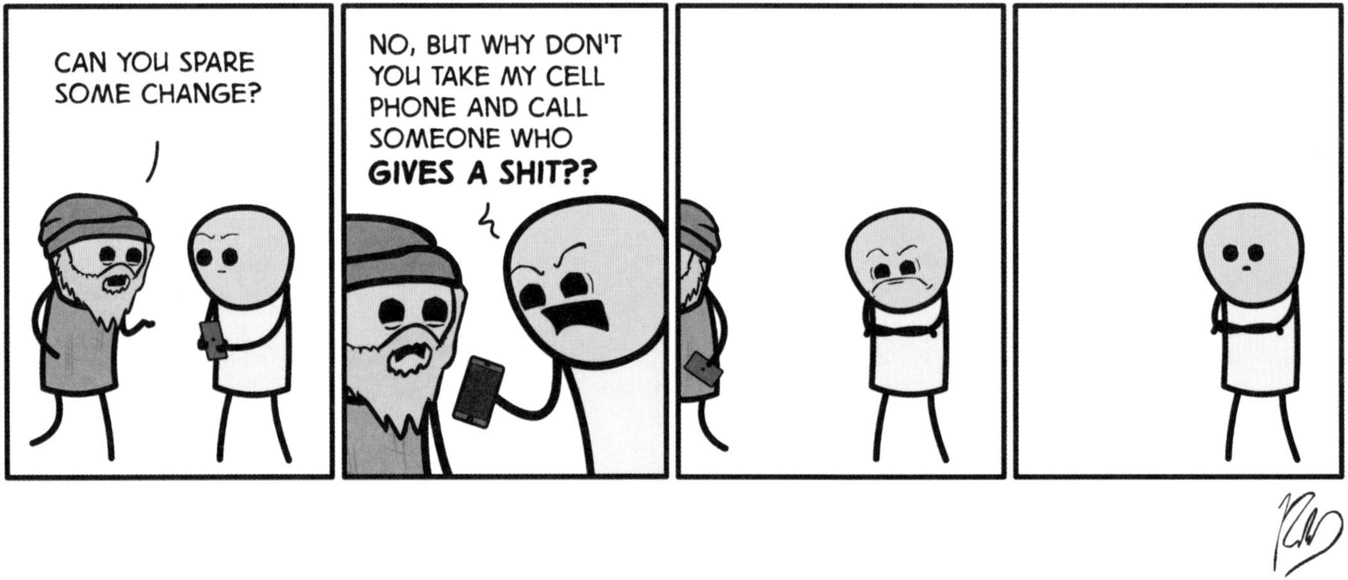
CAN YOU SPARE SOME CHANGE?
NO, BUT WHY DON'T YOU TAKE MY CELL PHONE AND CALL SOMEONE WHO **GIVES A SHIT??**

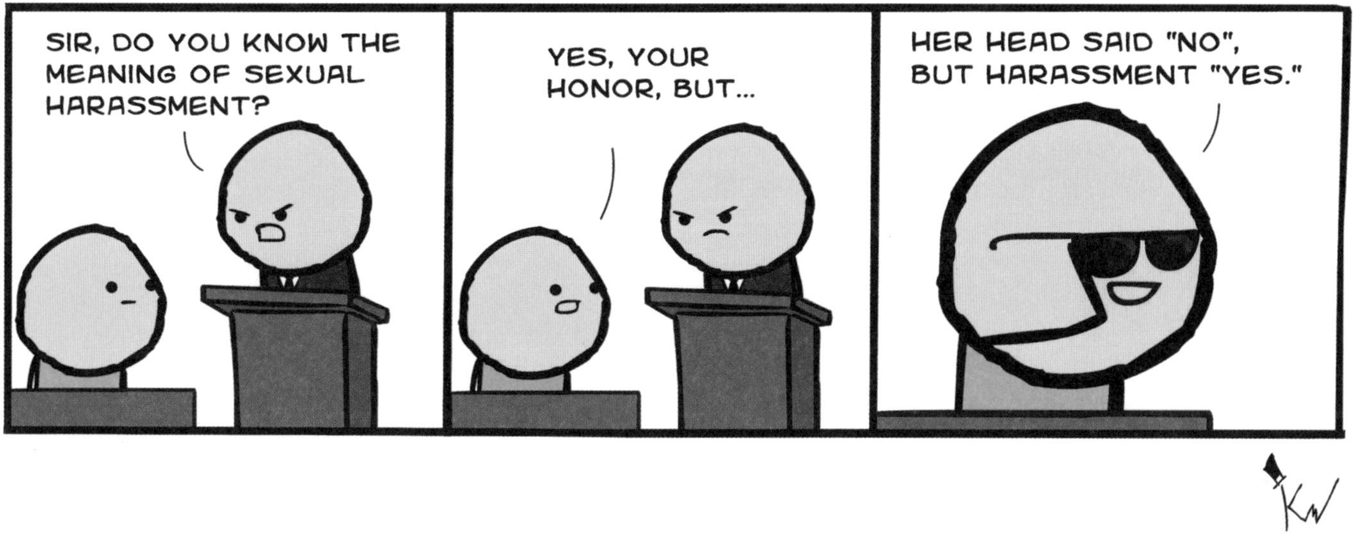
SIR, DO YOU KNOW THE MEANING OF SEXUAL HARASSMENT?
YES, YOUR HONOR, BUT...
HER HEAD SAID "NO", BUT HARASSMENT "YES."

I'M JUST NOT FEELING SEXY LATELY...
WHAT IF WE TRIED SOME STRIP TEASING?
OKAY.
HAHA, YOUR DICK IS SMALL.

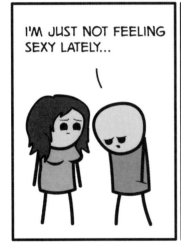

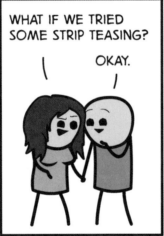

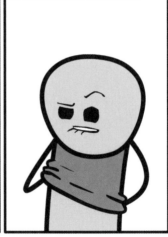

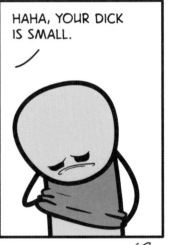

UH, HONEY? YOU'D BETTER TAKE A LOOK AT THIS! THERE ARE PEOPLE OUTSIDE OF OUR HOUSE!
MY GOD.
THERE'S 7.125 BILLION OF THEM!
LOCK
KW

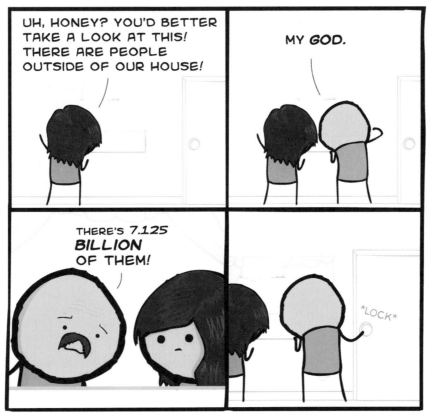

HEY, CAN I HAVE A PENNY TO SCRATCH THIS LOTTERY CARD? I'M HOPING TO WIN BIG BUCKS
I DON'T HAVE A PENNY, BUT I CAN GIVE YOU A MILLION DOLLARS IN CASH
AH, NEVERMIND THEN
Dave

WANNA WATCH SCHINDLER'S LIST ON BLU RAY?
NO THANKS... HOLOCAUST MOVIES JUST MAKE ME FEEL TERRIBLE.
YOU KNOW, 'CAUSE OF ALL THE JEWS *I'VE* KILLED.

Hot Cakes
7$
HEY, HOT CAKES!
Hot Cakes
7$
THAT'S RIGHT! BETTER BUY ONE NOW BEFORE THEY'RE SOLD OUT!
I WAS TALKING ABOUT YOU.

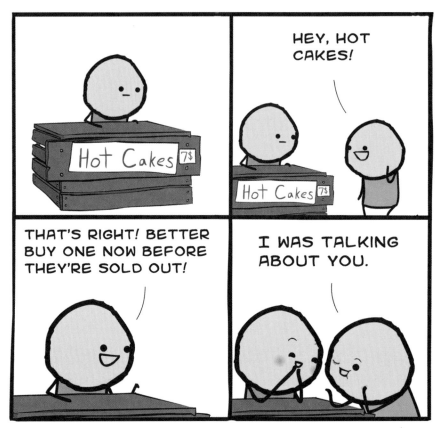

HEY, NICE HAT, MRS WILKINS!
THANKS!
IT'S MY HAT ACTUALLY!
I USE IT TO COVER MY HIDEOUS FEATURES
Dave

WE NEED TO TALK...
I'M LEAVING YOU.
WHAT!??
IT'S JUST... I DON'T
KNOW IF I CAN DATE
A DEAF PERSON.
WHAT!??

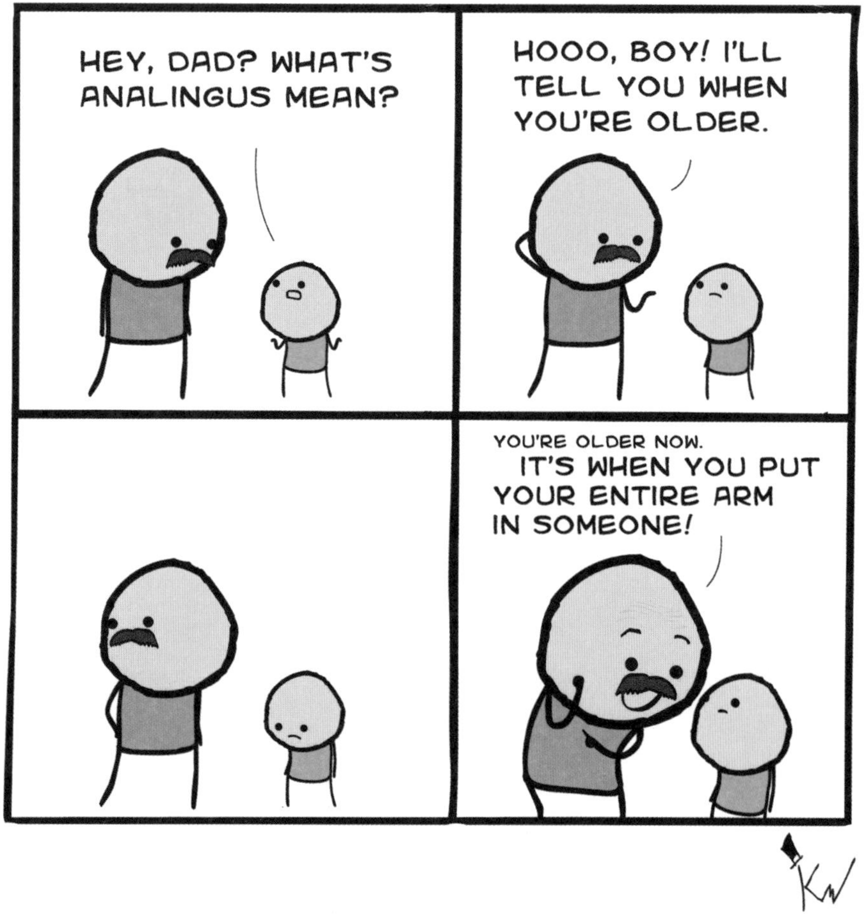
HEY, DAD? WHAT'S ANALINGUS MEAN?
HOOO, BOY! I'LL TELL YOU WHEN YOU'RE OLDER.
YOU'RE OLDER NOW.
IT'S WHEN YOU PUT YOUR ENTIRE ARM IN SOMEONE!

RACIST!
RACIST PIECE OF SHIT!
WHAT A DISGRACE!
GET OUTTA HERE, DICKWAD!
YOU'RE RIGHT, IT'S HARD BEING A BLACK MAN IN AMERICA
Dave

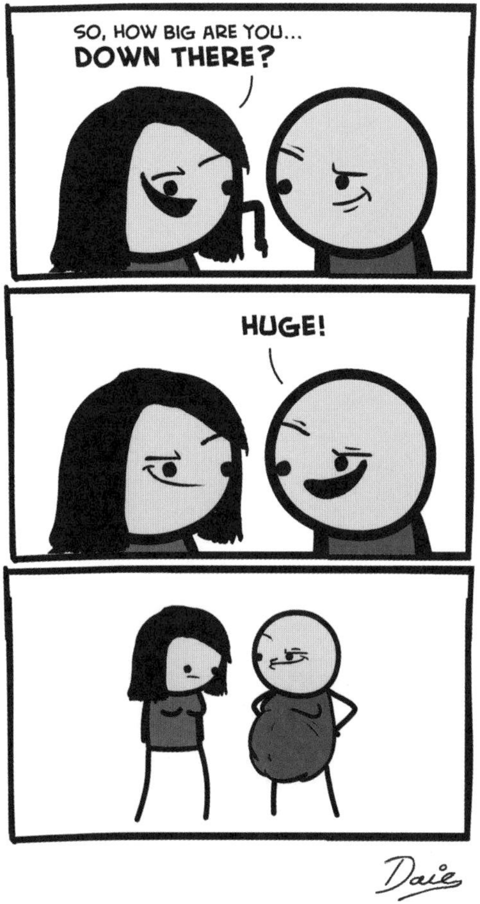
SO, HOW BIG ARE YOU... DOWN THERE?
HUGE!
Dale

Poetry Corner

Bingo Ben preferred the men,
His mum did not agree.
She squeezed her bosom in his face
And said "Whats wrong with me?"

Plough my fields,
And eat what it yields
Mother Earth said to her children
But instead they devoured
Every grass, tree, and flower
So Mother Earth had to kill them

Dumb Jimmy Bloo
Poured soup in a canoe
And took it out on water
His dick got burnt
And I slowly learnt
I shouldn't let him marry my daughter.

All around the cobbler's bench
The cobbler choked the weasel
The cobbler sighed in deep delight
Pop goes the weasel

Mary Jane, Mary Jane
What does your garden grow?
I answered my own question
I guess I'm really stoned.

Gerry was in Amsterdam
A town of much and plenty
Gerry found fuck all to do
Unless it was 4:20

Toss up my darling,
Toss him real high
Don't let his head, though
Hit the blue sky
Toss up my darling
Toss him indoors
Now his poor head
Is all over the floors

What you got there dear Mary, dear mary my dear?
Is that a bunch of berries, canaries, and pears?
"I got some from the flotsam down by the pier"
"Along with sailor fingers, teeth and some ears!"

Itsy bitsy spider climbed up the waterspout.

Down came the water and washed the spider out.

Fuck you, spider.

Hahahaha die, you piece of shit.

More water!

Little Tickle Bum liked to hide
In all the bushes and trees
He'd tickle the kids down at the park
Someone please call the police

The sheep goes blah
The cow says meh
The horse goes nah
The farmer says eh?

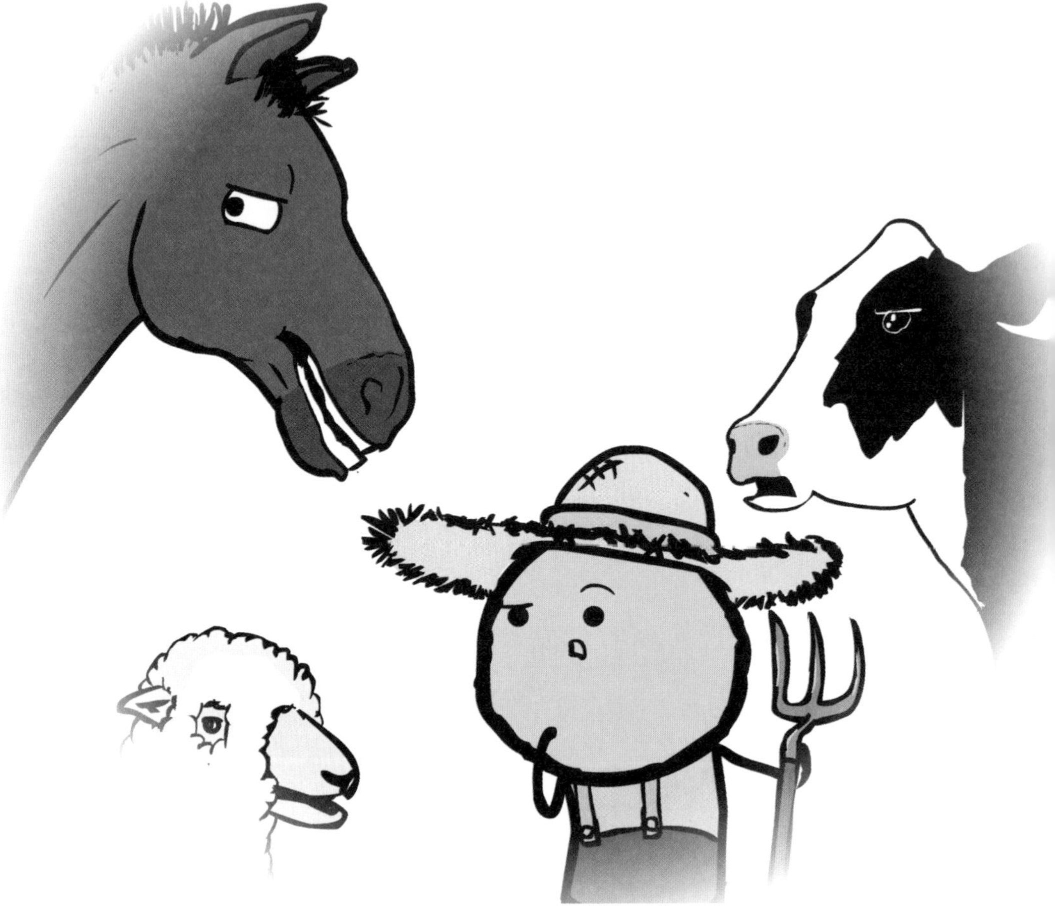

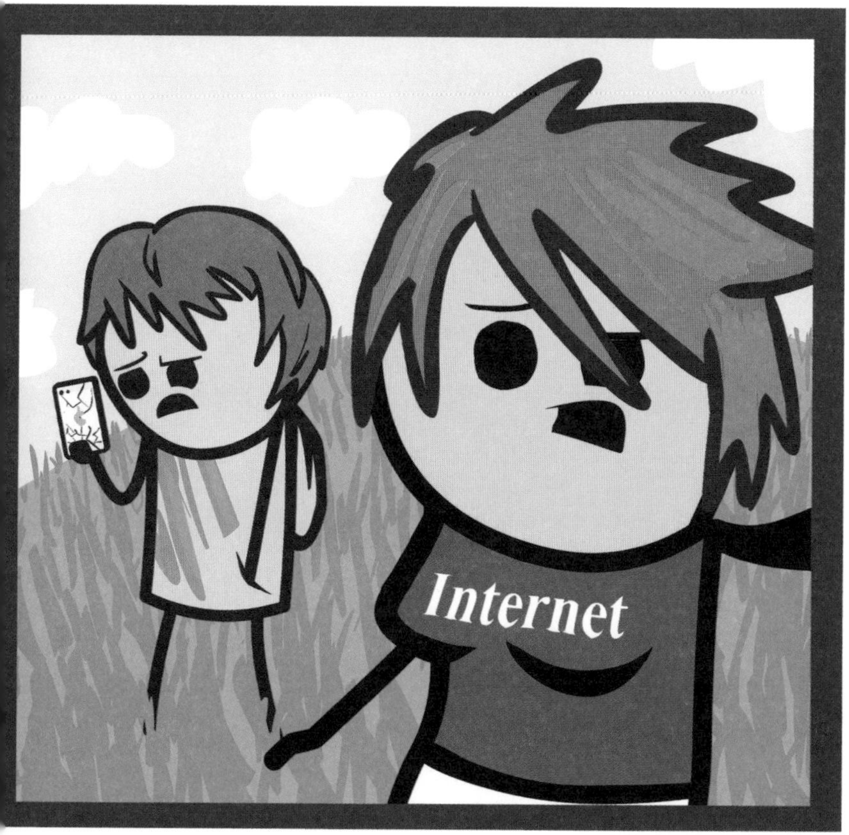
Internet

Jack and Jill went up the hill,
To get a selfie together.
Jack fell down and broke his phone
Jill went on tumblr. #whatever

Hurly Turly, a man so burly,
Could eat a horse and a half, surely
Could eat a dozen chicken curries,
Leaves you with the check 'cause he's in a hurry.

Georgie Porgie pudding pie
Kissed the girls and made them cry
Bound their mouth with silver tape
"Isn't this a lovely date?"

Little Bo Peep has lost her sheep,
Every sheep she's got.
But I won't be losing any sleep.
That lamb stew hits the spot.

Mango Munn, the chutney king
Put mango chutney in everything
He put it in hats and also in socks
I'd best invest in mango stocks!

Timmy Wimmy, yummy wummy
Dressed like a panda to be funny
He was irate when they forced him to mate
But he went with it just for the money

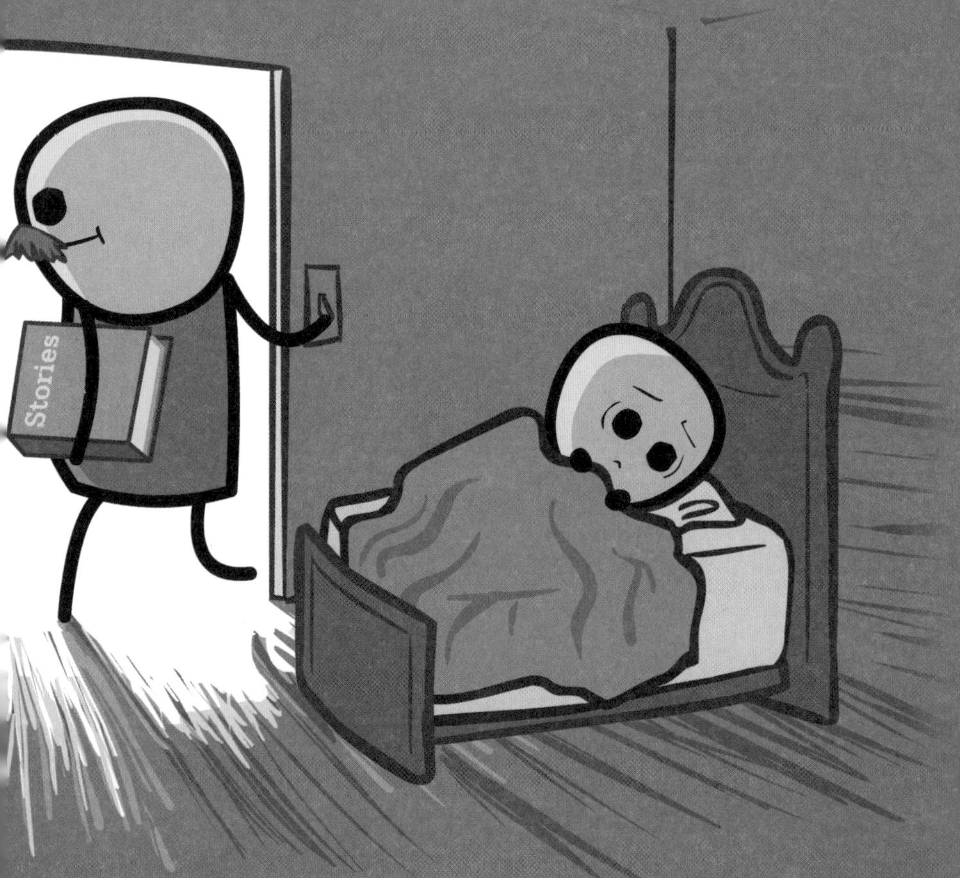
Stories

Little Miss Muffet
Sat on my face
It smelled like curds and whey
And that's the story
Of Little Miss Muffet
No more stories today.

Down by the docks

Is a little green croc

He's got a little sock

On his little green cock

Father's in the woods
searching for some goods
Brother's in the lake
catching all the snakes
mother left for cigarettes
they'll be back someday I bet

Mary Mary, quite contrarian,

Wants free healthcare,

But is libertarian.

Also vegetarian

But still eats fish

Mary, you're a crazy bitch

Samson Dee, the oldest tree
Proudly, he stood tall
He let the kids play on his trunk
And with his wooden balls
Samson Dee, you dirty tree
It's time to cut you down
I'll make a playground out of you
For all the kids in town

A man named Cohen
with no one who knows 'em
Went out to make a name
I'll write a poem!
Yeah that'll show 'em!
And surely i'll stake a claim!
The man named Cohen
Completed his poem
And set off to show it around
He wrote on his scrotum
Now everyone knows 'im
As Cohen: Best Scrotum in Town

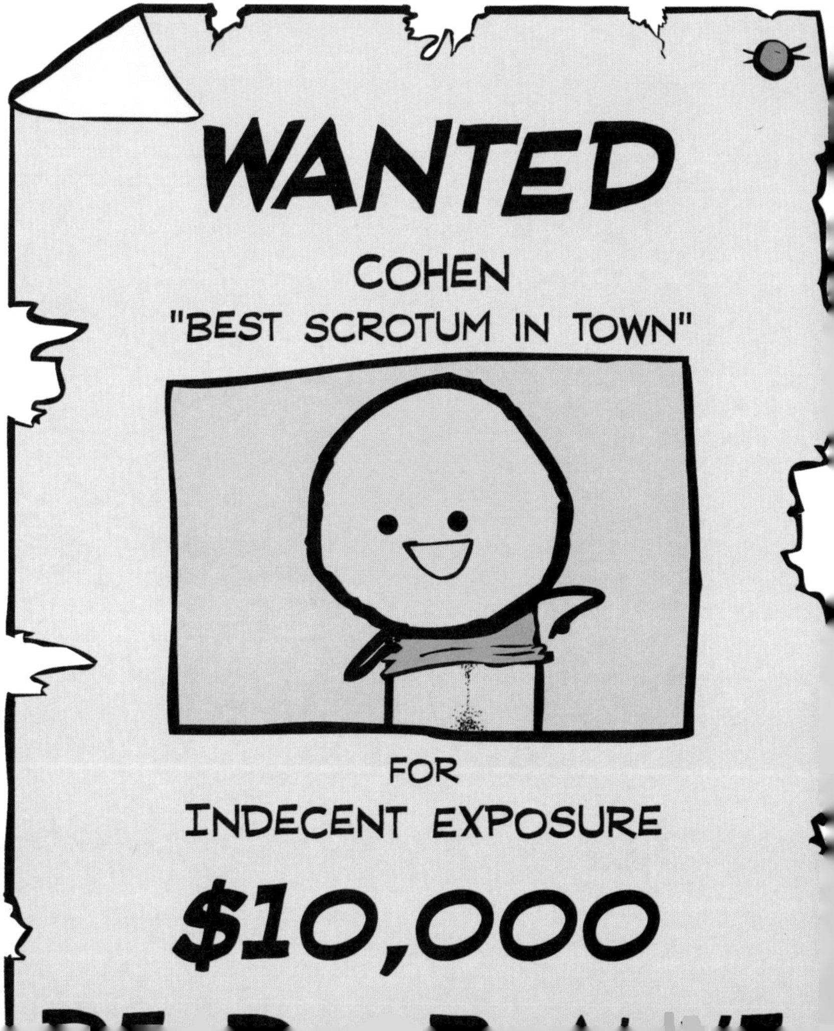
WANTED
COHEN
"BEST SCROTUM IN TOWN"
FOR
INDECENT EXPOSURE
$10,000

Rob, Bob and Bub
Three men in a tub
Scrubbity dubbity day.
Just Bob and Bub
Two men in a tub
And all of a sudden it's gay.

Pussycat, Pussycat

Where have you been?

I've been to London to visit the Queen

Pussycat Pussycat

What'd you do there?

I killed her family

And now I'm the heir

Old McDonald had a farm

E I E I O

And on that farm he had some slaves

UH OH UH OH NO

There once was a man named Blimerikoutov,
Whom nobody could make a limerick out of

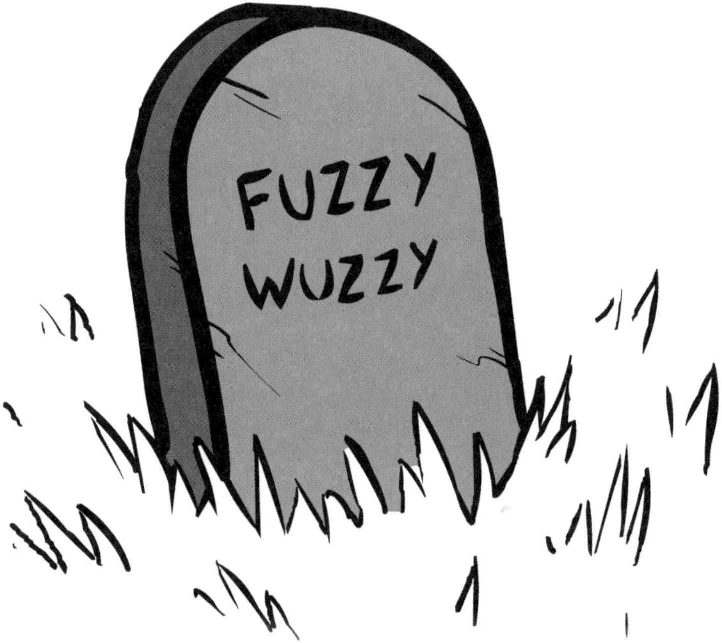
FUZZY
WUZZY

Fuzzy Wuzzy was a bear,
Fuzzy Wuzzy had no hair,
Fuzzy Wuzzy had stage three,
Fuzzy Wuzzy's in the cemetery.
Fuzzy Wuzzy wasn't very lucky, was he?

Richard Gnape, strong as an ape
Gonna avoid rhyming ape with rape
Shit now I've done it, there's no escape
ESCAPE. that would've been a good rhyme
I'll be sure to use that one next time.

Two robin redbreasts built their nest
In between two lovely breasts
The robin redbreasts rubbed the chest
Four robin, rubbin', throbbin' red breasts.